"Matt Woodley's *Folly of Prayer* puts language, meaning and practical helps around vital modes of prayer. The truest folly would be to ignore this biblical guidance in those murky, shifting waters of the soul's authentic connection with God!"

Mindy Caliguire

president, Soul Care, and author of *Discovering Soul Care, Soul Searching, Spiritual Friendship* and *Simplicity*

The Folly of Prayer

PRACTICING THE PRESENCE AND ABSENCE OF GOD

Matt Woodley

833 5938 9640

813862

An imprint of InterVarsity Press
Downers Grove, Illinois

InterVarsity Press
P.O. Box 1400, Downers Grove, IL 60515-1426
World Wide Web: www.ivpress.com
E-mail: email@ivpress.com

InterVarsity Press® is the book-publishing division of InterVarsity Christian Fellowship/USA®, a movement of students and faculty active on campus at hundreds of universities, colleges and schools of nursing in the United States of America, and a member movement of the International Fellowship of Evangelical Students. For information about local and regional activities, write Public Relations Dept., InterVarsity Christian Fellowship/USA, 6400 Schroeder Rd., P.O. Box 7895, Madison, WI 53707-7895, or visit the IVCF website at <www.intervarsity.org>.

Design: Cindy Kiple
Images: Kamil Vojnar/Trevillion Images

ISBN 978-0-8308-3712-0

Printed in the United States of America ∞

InterVarsity Press is committed to protecting the environment and to the responsible use of natural resources. As a member of Green Press Initiative we use recycled paper whenever possible. To learn more about the Green Press Initiative, visit <www.greenpressinitiative.org>.

Library of Congress Cataloging-in-Publication Data

Woodley, Matt.
The folly of prayer: practicing the presence and absence of God / Matthew Woodley.
p. cm.
Includes bibliographical references (p.) and index.
ISBN 978-0-8308-3712-0 (pbk.: alk. paper)
1. Prayer—Christianity. I. Title.
BV210.3.W66 2009
248.3'2—dc22

2009011674

P	18	17	16	15	14	13	12	11	10	9	8	7	6	5	4	3	2	1
Y	24	23	22	21	20	19	18	17	16	15	14	13	12	11	10	09		

CONTENTS

INTRODUCTION

REIMAGINING PRAYER

I prayed my first real prayer when I was nine years old. The Minnesota Vikings needed a little help to get into the playoffs, but the prospects weren't looking good. Down by one point toward the end of a critical regular-season game, the Vikings offense drove to their opponents' twenty-yard line. With a few seconds left, our field-goal kicker, Fred Cox, could chip it in and win the game. Freddie was the last of the straight-on toe kickers, so within forty yards he was unusually accurate. But still I couldn't watch. So I sat on the living room steps and prayed. Up to this point in my life, I hadn't asked God for anything. We hardly ever spoke to each other. But now I needed a big favor, so I fervently prayed, *God, just put it right down the middle.* And as I prayed, I listened to the television announcer give the details of that final play: "The kick is up, it's sailing . . . oh no, it's hooking wide right. Freddie Cox just missed the game-winning field goal. The Vikings have lost the game."

Freddie's career crashed, and my tender faith shattered. I didn't speak to God for another four years. When I finally did start talking with God again, I was a surly, unhappy, hotheaded teenager. I didn't enjoy life, and I resented God's existence. How could I trust a God who seemed bent on working against my happiness? So whenever anything negative occurred in my life, I would turn to God in "prayer"—that is, a string of God-directed expletives. One sunny July afternoon, while casually playing basketball in the driveway of our suburban home, my ball kept rolling under my parents' car, getting wedged against the muffler. After the fifth incident I looked up at the sky, shook my fist at God and screamed, "This was no accident you *bleep-bleep-bleep* God. I hate you! Why don't you just leave me alone?" I meant it. God didn't deserve my love or respect.

Since then, I've changed my mind about God. I don't believe in a God who jams basketballs under mufflers just to make me miserable. And I don't feel a need to curse at God. Now I believe in the God who is the source of true and lasting happiness. Obviously, this has changed my practice of prayer. A few years after my prayer-as-profanity exhibition, I knelt beside my bed and asked Jesus Christ to be my Lord and Savior. A year later someone gave me a handy pattern for prayer called ACTS. It outlined the four basic categories for prayer: Adoration, Confession, Thanksgiving and Supplication. It was a tidy summary that helped me broaden my prayer life. I could move beyond demanding field goals and expressing rage. For many years I stuck with this basic ACTS pattern of prayer.

Eventually, however, I started to notice that the Bible offers a much broader perspective on prayer. I still like the basic fourfold pattern, but I've also found other patterns for prayer right in the pages of the Bible. There is prayer as guttural groaning, when we come into God's presence and just ache and hurt. There is prayer as hearing God's heartbeat, as we simply rest in God's deep love for us. There is prayer as a long, slow journey, as we learn to wait on God's timetable for our lives.

In all, this book explores eleven paths or ways to pray, which have five things in common. First, each of these paths to prayer is deeply rooted in the Bible. The Bible is a sprawling book that appeals to our reason and our imagination. For key issues in theology or spirituality (such as sin or redemption or the character of God), it never presents just one image or picture. So it makes sense that the Bible would provide a rich array of colors and images and pictures for our prayer life. And that's exactly what we find. Every image flows from the deep and beautiful stream of the Bible's view of prayer.

Second, the prayer paths in this book engage us on an intellectual, emotional and relational level. God will crack our hearts wide open. We can't "groan" our prayers to God without accessing the grief and longings in our gut. We can't listen to God's heartbeat without feeling loved. We can't have an argument with God without getting angry. And we can't pray sacramentally without touching God's creation, the stuff of life—skin, trees, blood, bread and wine. These prayers require our entire being—our senses, our emotions and our brain—to show up and be present to God.

Third, the ways of praying presented in this book have sometimes been marginalized by contemporary Christ-followers. I'm not suggesting there's been a massive cover-up; sometimes we just don't know how to pray. Most of us have never been taught to pray by groaning in a Godward direction or by confronting God with a good argument or by paying attention to God's presence. We're unfamiliar with these ways of praying; we may not even consider them prayers at all. The chapters that follow intentionally explore these quiet, hidden, marginalized ways to know God more intimately.

Fourth, most of these paths to prayer will open our hearts to God and to other people. They will help us grow deep with God and then move us to display compassion for others. These marginal ways of praying will compel us to engage with marginal people—the desperate, the groaning, the victimized and the ignored. As we start to pray in a more full-bodied biblical way, God will open our eyes not only to his glory but also to the pain of the world around us.

And finally, there is a certain "folly" to prayer. Prayer isn't necessarily efficient or even comprehensible. Sometimes we feel and know the palpable presence of God, and we cry out, "Thank you!" At other times we experience more of God's haunting, mysterious, unpredictable absence, and we scream, "Where are you?" And we usually can't predict God's next move. In this sense, praying to our untamed God can be frustrating, perplexing and even agonizing. God will bathe us in ecstatic light and then seemingly abandon us in the dark. To be blunt, sometimes real prayer with the real God can drive us nuts!

But that's real life. Reality itself—from quarks and human cells to redwood forests and blue whales—is quirky and unpredictable, riddled with sharp edges and surprises and setbacks and strange events. So if God is real (and he is!), God will be characterized by the same things. After all, would we really want a completely predictable, unsurprising, smooth-edged God? I have a hunch we'd quickly fall asleep on God.

So the folly of prayer is sometimes painful and exasperating. But it's an encounter between the real God and the real us. I don't enjoy pain, confusion, failure and suffering. I've spent an enormous amount of energy trying to suppress the dark side of life. Unfortunately, if I try to shut down the neural pathways of pain, I will also shut down the pathways of deepest delight. The result: a numbed life. I've been there, but I'm not staying there. I want to face life head-on, with all its jagged edges of mystery, joy, longing and agony. This book is my journey to come alive and be present in one critical facet of my life: my prayer life.

My prayer is that my journey will help you come alive to God and to others like never before.

1

PRAYER AS GUTTURAL GROANING

Recently a good friend of mine, a young and brilliant student, sent me the following entry from her blog:

> I wonder about faith a lot. I wonder if there's a God, if love is just an exchange of pheromones, and if anything really happens after a human body dies. Sometimes I go to church, but sometimes I roll my eyes when people talk about religion. Sometimes I tell myself not to care, and sometimes it's impossible not to.
>
> I gave up reading the news for awhile. It seemed so depressing—people are always dying, killing each other, bombing a streetcar or a train, shooting at schoolgirls. . . . When I read the news, every fiber of my being cries out for a god who hears and answers prayer, a god who knows each one of us by name. But these news reports—and sometimes my own life experiences—seem to reproach me, even as I cry out, as if I should know better. They seem to say, it's so obvious you're crying out to no one but yourself.
>
> And yet. There are times when I'm not so sure. These times are personal—maybe an unexpected act of kindness, a string of answered prayers, the sudden glimpse of a glorious sunset.

Maybe they mean nothing. But there are times when I feel, deep down, that God exists and God loves—me.

Her blog entry is anguished and honest, heartbreaking and hopeful. Part of me wanted to hug her and part of me wanted to advise her. I love advice (giving it, that is), and I can usually slip my smooth religious counsel into this tidy one-liner: "If you would just do/believe/start A, then you would soon discover/experience/learn B." I wanted to provide the A and B so I could scoop the anguish from her soul and help her pray better. But I couldn't find the right words. Besides, my friend is too smart and too honest—and I like her too much—for a quick formula.

And then it hit me: maybe my friend's anguished entry was already a prayer. Maybe there are times when we pray and don't even know we're praying, when the doubt and anguish are lodged so deep within us that we can't find the words. So we just ache. And we groan. And we ooze with the pain of life. And maybe God hears the ugly groans and changes the ooze into poetry.

THE STORY OF GROANING

Does that sound too good to be true? I don't think so. The Bible is a God-centered, Jesus-glorifying, Spirit-empowered story, but even so, it constantly honors human suffering. It teaches us how to groan, and then it tells us that God validates our deepest groaning. Sometimes we just hurt and we can't find the words to express our pain. We can't explain it, heal it, overcome it, solve it or blunt it. So we just sit and groan in a Godward direction. In these situations, the groans themselves can become messy-eloquent offerings to God. And in the midst of these groans, God hears us and holds us, and then he helps us em-

brace our fellow groaners.

The first groan mentioned in the Bible occurs in Exodus 2:23, when "the Israelites groaned in their slavery." They had lived as slaves in Egypt for four hundred years. The children of Israel ached in body and spirit. Their sons were dying, and their backs were breaking. The Egyptians made their lives bitter with hard service in mortar and brick (Exodus 1:11-14). It was ruthless and wrong, and they couldn't take it anymore. So they groaned to God. It wasn't pretty. It didn't look like a typical church prayer meeting. But apparently God labeled it as a "real prayer" because "God heard their groaning and he remembered his covenant with Abraham, with Isaac and with Jacob" (Exodus 2:24). In other words, the entire exodus story, the greatest event in the history of the Jewish people, was set in motion not by a polished, sophisticated prayer but by a series of groans that bled out of their collective gut.

From that point on, the Israelites continued their groaning. Job prayed his groans: "My groans pour out like water" (Job 3:24). David prayed his groans: "I am worn out from groaning" (Psalm 6:6); "I groan in anguish of heart" (Psalm 38:8); "I remembered you, O God, and I groaned" (Psalm 77:3). The prophets prayed their groans: "My groans are many and my heart is faint" (Lamentations 1:22).

Even after the new and final exodus event—the cross and resurrection of Jesus—Christ-followers keep groaning. Paul groans and raises these groan-prayers to a new level of depth and beauty. He mentions the "groans that words cannot express" (Romans 8:26). For Paul, these guttural groans are an appropriate response to life in a fallen and flawed world. That's Paul's dense statement in Romans 8:18-25.

This statement follows three simple movements: First, the world is bent, flawed, tainted, broken and maimed: "For the creation was subjected to frustration"(Romans 8:20). Everything that exists reflects something about this bentness. Second, one day God will straighten this bent world. God is already healing our bentness, and one day he will bring everything under Jesus' lordship (see Ephesians 1:10). In Paul's soaring words, "the creation itself will be liberated from its bondage to decay and brought into the glorious freedom of the children of God" (Romans 8:21). Third, Jesus is alive and at work in the world even today, but he isn't finished with his healing work. So we're caught in the tension of bentness and healing, brokenness and redemption, sin and glory. As Paul says elsewhere, "Meanwhile we groan, longing to be clothed with our heavenly dwelling" (2 Corinthians 5:2).

Groaning occurs in the gap between what is (our nakedness) and what will be (our party clothes). We ache and grope for redemption, for beauty, for resolution (that's why our best stories are always redemption stories); but we aren't there yet. We're standing naked, and we should be and we will be clothed in our wedding garb. We should be and we will be fully redeemed, transformed into glorious creatures, but we haven't arrived there yet.[1] We're caught in this painful tension. According to the poet Franz Wright, we are the only animal that can contemplate suicide while we go for a walk in the park.[2]

MUTING OUR GROANS

Of course, that doesn't mean it's easy to face the groans in our hearts. In a pitiable scene from a *Seinfeld* episode, Kramer asks George, "Do you ever yearn, George?" George tries to brush it off, but Kramer won't let up: "Do you ever yearn, George?" "What do you mean?" George asks. Once again, Kramer demands an answer: "Do you ever yearn?" George is getting annoyed, so he finally concedes, "No, I never yearn; I just crave."

But according to the biblical story, we live in a yearning, aching universe, not just a craving universe. But like George, most of us have a huge problem with this: it hurts to groan; it aches to ache. It's little wonder, then, that human beings tend to deny and blunt the pain of groaning. The brilliant mathematician-philosopher Blaise Pascal frequently mentioned our need for "diversions," those activities and habits that mute our groaning. In his *Pensées* he wrote, "As men are not able to fight against death, misery and ignorance [i.e., all the things that make us groan in this bent world], they have taken it into their heads, in order to be happy, not to think of them at all."[3] As a result, we've developed entire industries to help us numb the ache in our hearts. So many voices in our culture scream, "Buy this, try that, get this, have this experience, travel here, and you'll stop groaning."

Many of us also grew up in church or family systems that taught us to deny the ache. So with glossy brochures and slick websites, churches promise us: "Try our worship services, follow our program, listen to our sermons, and God will pluck the groaning out of your heart. All of these happy, groan-free faces can't be wrong." Somewhere we bought the lie that we could live without pain, that we could stuff it, numb it, medicate it, blunt it, or stiff-arm it.

And it works—sort of. Unfortunately, this approach doesn't just numb the anguish of living in a fallen world; it also numbs the glory of living in a redemption-charged world. It shuts down both circuits because they run along the same pathways. In the biblical story, prayer doesn't resolve the tension of living in a fallen world; it intensifies the ache. Prayer makes us groan louder, not softer. Groaning gets us in touch with the pain and the hope, the ache and the glory, the deep sadness and the nearly unbearable joy of life in a Christ-redeemed world. Groaning is a sure sign that we're facing reality, with all its beautiful-ragged edges. It shows that we're connected to the whole creation. Christians should be the best and loudest groaners in the world. We are the leaders of the great cosmic groan chorus.[4]

So here's ground rule number one for life on planet earth: everyone groans; no one escapes. As a matter of fact, Paul said "the whole creation" groans (Romans 8:22). On a huge, abstract level I clearly understand Paul's point: we all live in a fallen world, a world marred and maimed by our revolt against God's good intentions for his creation. Everything that *is* is tainted by the Fall. But since "the creation" also consists of specific things and particular creatures, I still wonder what Paul meant. Do elephants groan? Apparently they do grieve when they lose their mates. Do dragonfly nymphs groan? Do birch trees groan every autumn as their leaves turn gold, shimmer in the breeze and then plummet to the ground? When my beagle, Dwight, waits for me to come home from work, does he ever groan? I know he craves (especially food), but does he also yearn and ache?

I don't know, but I do know that even followers of Jesus, those who have "the firstfruits of the Spirit," those who are saved in hope of redemption, still "groan inwardly" (Romans 8:23). Sometimes I'd like God to grant me an exemption from this great cosmic groaning, but he hasn't and he won't. I will groan along with the rest of creation until the day I die.

Recently, during one of the most painful seasons of my life, all kinds of friends gave me advice. Some of my Christians friends urged me to seek the Lord and find joy in the midst of trials. One friend pointedly asked, "Why don't you ask your doctor for antidepressants?" Finally I started to tell all my well-meaning friends, "Look, I'm not opposed to medication, and I'm thankful for the advice, but I just need to be sad right now. Something precious has broken in my heart, and I can't fix it. So I ache. For now, would you let me join the rest of creation in groaning my prayers toward God?"

TRUSTING THE GROANING GOD

So here's the utterly astounding truth about our groan-prayers: God hears them. Neuroscientists have proven that mothers can identify their newborn's unique cry in a matter of minutes after birth. Her baby's groan is hard-wired into her brain. In the same way, even in the vast, dark space of the cosmos and in the teeming mass of the earth's 6,000,000,000-plus people, God can locate me based on my unique groans. It's hard-wired into God's nature and character.

But it gets even more amazing: God not only hears my groans, God groans within me. For "the Spirit himself intercedes for us with groans that words cannot express" (Romans 8:26). And the Spirit helps us in our weakness because sometimes "we do not know what we ought to pray for." Even when we don't have the words, even when we don't have a clue where to start, even when our lives are splitting wide open with the anguish of this bent world, even then the Holy Spirit groans within us and for us. In other words, a quiet conversation continues deep within the heart of every follower of Jesus: God prays to God *for us* "with groans that words cannot express."

Not only that, in Jesus Christ, God also prays and groans *with* us. God in the flesh, Jesus enters into our groaning. If humans groan on this bent planet, and if Jesus wanted to be made like his brothers and sisters in all things, then Jesus chooses to become the ultimate groaner (see Hebrews 2:14-18). So in John 11, as Jesus stood beside his friend's grave, he wept. In this scene, death has intruded the good creation, wreaking havoc. One day death, the last enemy, will be vanquished, but not yet. So Jesus stands in solidarity with us and groans for what is broken and shattered. Then as Jesus hung on the cross for our sins, he also dangled and groaned between what is and what will be.

So based on all of this biblical theology, here's a tiny picture of your prayer life: imagine that you're sitting on a park bench in mid-May. The sun is shining, cardinals are singing, and apple trees are budding, but your heart is heaving with a thick sadness. Something is broken in your world, and you can't fix it. Choose your pain:

You've been diagnosed with cancer.
You lost your job.
You flunked the entrance exam.
Your child's life is in shambles.
A friend is moving and you already miss him or her.
Your spouse/boyfriend/girlfriend is leaving you.
You're just sad and depressed.
Other.

You try to pray, and you want to pray. You stammer, but the words get lodged in your throat. As a friend of mine said regarding the pain of a wayward child, "When I try to pray about it, it's like trying to pick up a fallen electrical wire. It's too hot; I can't even touch it." All you can do is turn Godward and groan your anguish. But according to the Bible's view of our prayer life, your God-directed groans are connecting you to God. God says, "Because of the . . . groaning of the needy, I will now arise" (Psalm 12:5). The Spirit who dwells within you is interceding to God the Father about you. Jesus who stands besides you is praying to God the Father for you. Groaning—the most primal, inarticulate and guttural form of communication—is imbued with trinitarian wonder. Groaning is God's prayer within us.

THE AMAZING, HEART-OPENING, SOUL-ENRICHING POWER OF GROANING

In a startling way, our willingness to groan actually opens our hearts. By fleeing the ache of this fallen world, by manufacturing diversions, by demanding that God and others remove our groans, we contract our souls. But groaning our prayers to God expands and opens our hearts. Specifically, prayer as guttural groaning opens our hearts to God's comfort, God's hope and God's compassion.

Groaning opens our hearts to comfort. First, groaning opens our hearts to God's comfort. In her classic work on trauma and recovery, Harvard psychiatrist Judith Herman contends, "The ordinary response to atrocities is to banish them from consciousness. Certain violations of the social order are too terrible to utter aloud: this is the meaning of the word unspeakable."[5] In other words, the standard message we often give suffering people is, "Please don't groan around us—at least not too loudly. Keep it quiet; keep it under control." I can't remember the number of times I've invalidated fellow groaners, leaving them comfortless and alone.

In contrast, the God we approach through Jesus Christ validates the most intense groans that issue from our worst atrocities. God doesn't know the word *unspeakable*. God even provides us with an entire biblical book, the book of Lamentations, that is devoted to validating our groans. Tucked into the middle of the Bible, this tiny text is so hidden that we usually miss it. Indeed, it isn't a pretty book. It's raw and jagged. On one level, it's the private journal of a man who has encountered profound grief and suffering. He's trying to speak the unspeakable; he's trying to make sense of the nonsensical. The text is one long groan-prayer.

How did these unspeakable events develop? In 587 B.C., after a two-year siege, the Babylonian army broke through the walls of Jerusalem, the capital city. They invaded the city, destroyed the temple, captured and executed the political leaders, and then forced most of the inhabitants to start marching six hundred miles into exile. The loss was devastating. They lost homes, jobs, families, worship centers, political leaders and an entire way of life. As he wrote this book, the author-poet-storyteller was still in shock.

So Lamentations trains us to take the grief lodged in our heart and in creation itself and groan it in a Godward direction. The book begins with the Hebrew word *ekah*. Most English versions translate it as "how," but it's difficult to convey the sense of pathos in the word. *Ekah* is a cry of lament that lodges in the throat, stuffed down with horror and sorrow. In the Hebrew Bible this one word is indented and then placed on a line by itself with a space after it. "*Ekah!*"—and then there is silence and white space. A gut-wrenching groan, and then nothing: unspeakable.

Throughout the book, in emotionally charged poetry, God trains us to grieve. The poetry of Lamentations is in the shape of five acrostics that begin with the first Hebrew letter and then walk through all twenty-two letters of the Hebrew alphabet. Thus, it covers our groans "from A to Z" not once but five times.

Nearly every verse throbs with pain. "How deserted lies the city, once so full of people! . . . Bitterly she weeps at night, tears are upon her cheeks" (Lamentations 1:1-2). We notice that the first task in this prayer is to see reality, to view the tension between what is and what will be, and then to keep looking at it without denial or distortion. And what the writer sees makes his heart leak with grief. Once again, prayer doesn't remove the ache in our hearts; it intensifies our joys and our groans. Prayer "un-numbs" the heart.

And how does God respond to our messy groan-prayers? He lets us feel, and he lets us groan. A consistent theme runs through Lamentations: the search for a comforter.

> "Among all her lovers there is none to comfort her." (Lamentations 1:2)
>
> "This is why I weep and my eyes overflow with tears. No one is near to comfort me, no one to restore my spirit." (Lamentations 1:16)
>
> "Zion stretches out her hands, but there is no one to comfort her." (Lamentations 1:17)

"People have heard my groaning, but there is no one to comfort me." (Lamentations 1:21)

Throughout the Bible, God becomes the ultimate comforter for people in grief and anguish. "The God of all comfort" validates our groaning and then "comforts us in all our troubles" (2 Corinthians 1:3-4). God becomes the comforter, the one who holds us. The Bible does not provide a comprehensive "answer" for suffering, but it does promise us God's personal presence in and through suffering. Someday this personal presence will be so real and palpable that all the sadness and tears will be banished. Suffering will end. God will heal this bent and broken planet. But now we live in the tension between full redemption and our fallen state. We ache, but in the midst of our groans, even because of our groans, our hearts open to the presence of the God of all comfort.

Child psychiatrist Dr. Bruce Perry recounts the amazing story of a foster mother named "Mama P." Dr. Perry and his team of psychiatrists, psychologists, pediatricians and medical students had descended on the case of a troubled boy named Robert. Robert's mom was a cocaine-addicted prostitute who routinely abused Robert. After removing Robert from his home, social workers shuffled him between nine residences and diagnosed him with a dozen psychological disorders. His case seemed hopeless until Mama P. became his comforter.

During a consultation, Mama P., a large and powerful woman, accosted Dr. Perry: "So, Dr. Perry, what can you do to help my baby?" Dr. Perry immediately suggested medication, but Mama P. interrupted and firmly said, "You will not use drugs on my baby. My baby does not need drugs!"

Surprised and confused, Dr. Perry asked her, "Mama P., how do you help 'your baby'?"

"I just hold him and rock him. I just love him. At night when he wakes up scared and wanders the house, I just put him in bed next to me, rub his back and sing a little and he falls asleep."

"What seems to calm him down when he gets upset during the day?"

"Same thing. I just put everything down and hold him and rock him in the chair. Doesn't take too long, poor thing."

Recalling Robert's immature, rage-filled behavior, Dr. Perry asked, "But Mama P., when he acts like that, don't you ever get frustrated and angry?"

"Do you get angry with a baby when a baby fusses?" she asked. "No. That is what babies do. Babies do the best they can and we always forgive them if they mess, if they cry, if they spit up on us."[6]

In the Bible, God is like Mama P.—fierce, strong, tender and wise. The Bible describes God in the following "Mama P.–like" words: "Can a mother forget the baby at her breast, and have no compassion on the child she has borne? Though she may forget, I will not forget you!" (Isaiah 49:15). God the Father is also the God of all motherlike comfort. God knows we'll fuss and cry and mess and spit. The groans will gurgle up from our gut. But in a surprising way, these groans become the conduit for God's comfort. As we groan, the God of all comfort, the God and Father of our Lord Jesus Christ, simply holds us and says, "There, there, child. Go ahead and groan now. Let me hold you and rock you and pour my comfort into your heart."

Groaning opens our hearts to hope. A lifestyle of groaning prayers also opens our hearts to hope. That is the thesis of Paul's argument in Romans 8:24-25. Groaning opens our hearts to more hope, and hope opens our hearts to more groaning. In this life, groaning and hope will remain tangled together like two wild vines. Honestly, sometimes it's better not to hope. As one of the characters says in the movie *Shawshank Redemption,* "Hope is a dangerous thing. It can drive us insane." Hopelessness closes the human heart, but once you start hoping, you become vulnerable. Hope is a choice to live a non-numbing life. Once you start hoping, your heart starts bursting with longing—because now you have something that you want. And the longing and groaning can hurt.

Up until I was twelve years old, I had never been to a Minnesota Vikings football game. As a young boy, few things were more thrilling than sitting in my cozy living room and watching the Vikings play on a frigid Sunday afternoon in December. I could safely watch fifty-five thousand Minnesota fans dressed in snowmobile suits, sipping coffee from their plaid thermoses, filling the stadium air with their warm breath. I was a spectator and never hoped to see a real Vikings game.

But then one day in early August my dad announced that he had purchased two sets of season tickets for the Vikings games. My two brothers and I would "draft" two games apiece. And I would actually attend a real Vikings game—in the cold, with real men (and a few brave women), drinking from a plaid thermos, sitting in the vastness of the Hubert Humphrey Stadium. Now I had hope.

What do you think hope does to a child's heart? Oh, hope is good! Hope sets your heart pounding with more delight and adventure than you ever thought possible. But hope also opens your heart to the ache of yearning and longing. In some ways my life was less painful before I had the hope of attending a Vikings game. I was content to sit in my warm but dull suburban living room without setting one foot outside on a December day in Minnesota. But now I had hope, and it split me wide open.

True biblical hope eventually leads to fulfillment. As the Bible promises, "hope [as opposed to wishful thinking] does not disappoint us" (Romans 5:5). I attended my two games. I put on my snowsuit and sat in the bleachers in weather cold enough to crack my lips. But hope didn't resolve the tension; it intensified the ache. Hope always draws a picture of a beautiful and good future and then says, "It's coming! It's coming! It will be yours! The One who promised it is faithful and true, but you'll have to wait for it." So we groan as we wait for the glory to come. Hope and groaning thrive together.

My friend Theresa displays this deep combination of hope and groaning. She's spent most of her life in a wheelchair, and at this point in her life, she's unable to drive or work. She's a full-grown adult with a sharp mind and a quick wit, but she's completely dependent on her parents' care. She knows the broad and glorious promises of Scripture. She knows that one day Christ will transform her broken body into the likeness of his resurrection body (see Philippians 3:21). But as she waits for the full redemption of her body, this glorious hope causes her to groan even more. The hope is so good, so tantalizing, that she can *almost* grab it and taste it. But for now it's out of her reach, so she groans to have it. Our church needs Theresa. She's a leader in our groan chorus. Without her we might forget that hope and groaning go together, that hope intensifies our groaning.

Followers of Jesus feel that this groaning makes our lives deeper and richer. The brilliant fourth-century writer St. Augustine claimed, "It is yearning that makes the heart deep." *Desiderium sinus cordis.* Peter Brown, in his study of the life and spirituality of Augustine, captured Augustine's blend of groaning and hope:

> [Augustine] is a man who has realized that he was doomed to remain incomplete in his present existence, that what he wished for most ardently would never be more than a hope, postponed to a final resolution of all tensions, far beyond this life. Anyone who thought otherwise, he felt, was either morally obtuse or a doctrinaire. All a man could do was to "yearn" for this absent perfection, to feel its loss intensely, to pine for it. . . . [He was] defined by his tension towards something else, by his capacity for faith, for hope, for longing, to think of himself as a wanderer seeking a country that is always distant, but made ever-present to him by the quality of the love that "groans" for it.[7]

In Augustine's own words of groaning and hoping, he cried out, "Let me leave them outside, breathing into the dust, and filling their eyes with earth, and let me enter into my chamber and sing my songs of love to Thee, groaning with inexpressible groaning in my distant wandering, and remembering Jerusalem with my heart stretching upwards in longing for it: Jerusalem my Fatherland, Jerusalem who is my mother."[8]

For Augustine, like Paul, groaning engenders hope, and hope engenders groaning. As we dangle between agony and glory, between a sin-hardened world and a Christ-charged cosmos, our groans do not diminish us; they expand our hearts with hope. And then the vulnerability of our hope opens our hearts to more groaning.

Groaning opens our hearts to compassion. Prayer as guttural groaning also opens our hearts to a deep compassion for others. We begin to embrace the pain of our fellow groaners. As God fills us with his comfort, sometimes the best thing we can do is to *be* the presence of God's comfort to others.

Being present to others in pain—without fixing or lecturing or advising or even "helping"—is a rare and precious skill. Most of us want to give answers and solutions. Certainly there is a time to help and advise. But trained in the school of guttural groaning, we slowly learn the art of *being* with others rather than just *doing* things for others. At times just sitting beside a hurting person and groaning together is the best prayer we can offer.

Sometimes this ministry of shared groaning is simple and quiet. After author Joe Bayly buried his second son, he told the following story: "I was sitting torn by grief. Someone came and talked to me of God's dealings, of why it happened, of hope beyond the grave. He talked constantly, he said things I knew were true. I was unmoved, except to wish he'd go away. He finally did. Another came and sat beside me. He didn't ask any leading questions. He just sat beside me for an hour and more, listened when I said something, answered briefly, prayed simply, and left. I was moved. I was comforted. I hated to see him go."[9] Joe Bayly needed someone who could quietly *be* with him, providing a ministry of shared groaning. When it's given in the power of the Holy Spirit, this shared groaning ushers us into the presence of the God of all comfort.

Our mutual groaning doesn't always have to be quiet; sometimes our mutual groaning is loud and unruly. Last year three women showed up to pray for a friend of mine who was facing surgery and depression. She had requested prayer from these "praying Pentecostals." The three women talked to her for a few minutes, then they brought her into our church basement and started their little prayer meeting. I tried not to listen, but I couldn't help it. They were loud. These women knew how to groan! The three of them moaned their prayers to God with a fierceness that startled me.

I'm used to neat, placid, well-organized prayer meetings. Everyone takes a turn, like customers take a number at the deli counter. These women didn't take numbers; they all prayed at the same time. They weren't polite or placid or well-organized. They moaned together like three wounded lionesses. O how they groaned to their Father in heaven! I sure didn't want to interrupt. How do you stop a trio of wounded lionesses? They might have mauled me.

After thirty minutes of loud, fierce groaning, they stopped; then they quietly slipped out the back door. Things were quiet again, but I'll never forget what those women taught me about prayer. I've read profound writings by the great masters of Christian prayer. I've preached eloquent sermons on the theology of prayer. I'm even writing a book on prayer! But I've never prayed like those lionesses. I've never groaned with a reckless fierceness on behalf of someone else. By the time they left, I needed to get on my knees and cry out to Jesus, "Teach [me] to pray" (Luke 11:1)!

Ah, I'm learning to groan well. Indeed, it hurts to groan. It hurts to feel the pain in my heart and the agony of this fallen world. But it's real life. I'm learning that groaning does deepen our heart. And I'm listening to the God who tells me, "Groan away, my child. Groan well. Groan loudly. Groan as much as you want. One day the groaning will end, the weeping will end, the hurting will end. I will wipe every tear from your eye. But for now plunge into the groans of this world. I am with you. I am groaning in you and beside you. You are never alone."

2

PRAYER AS SKIN, TREES, BLOOD, BREAD AND WINE

This past summer I joined forces with fifteen men and two women for an intense game of church softball against our archrivals, "The Lutheran Psalms." For ninety minutes, we exerted our bodies, throwing, catching, running, sliding, sweating and yelling. As usual, the "Psalms" pummeled us, but at least they beat us on a beautiful summer evening. When the game ended, we lined up to shake hands with the more talented "Psalms" before gathering around our own bench, slapping each other's backs, guzzling cold water and admiring a gorgeous sunset. As we packed up our gear, one of my teammates yelled, "Hey, guys, let's thank God for the game. Okay now, everyone get quiet, close your eyes, and be still so we can pray."

So we all dutifully stopped talking, bowed our heads and closed our eyes. As we tried to focus on the prayer, a gaggle of geese honked over our heads. The scent of freshly mown grass filled our nostrils. I could hear some oak leaves rustling in the cool evening breeze. So midway through the prayer, I couldn't take it anymore: I cheated and opened my eyes. After all, for ninety minutes we had been in contact with the earth all around us, enjoying God's creation. Our bodies were immersed in dirt and grass and summer heat. I peeked because I wanted to pray like I had just played—with my eyes wide open to the beauty all around me.

I mention this story because many of us have developed a distorted assumption about prayer: in order to be really "spiritual" we must separate ourselves from the material world. God is a spirit, right? Therefore, connecting with God on a deeper level implies disconnecting from the physical stuff around us. So if you want to pray, be still and close your eyes. Turn inward. Don't touch. Don't smell. Use your brain but not your skin or nose. Don't get distracted by oak leaves rustling in the wind or geese honking overhead or the scent of freshly mown grass. Prayer is a "spiritual" experience.

From a biblical perspective this assumption is dead wrong. Prayer is not just a spiritual experience. In a fully biblical way of praying, we don't pray better by becoming more spiritual; we pray better by becoming more physical. Throughout the Bible, God is more or less telling us, "Look at that. Taste this. Smell this. Touch that. Move your body this way." I'm convinced that this physical, earthy, sensual (i.e., utilizing all of our senses) path to prayer will deepen our connection to God. And it's also the easiest and most practical path to prayer explored in this book.

PRAYING SACRAMENTALLY

Throughout the centuries the church has used a word for the concrete objects, signs and symbols used in this physical way of praying: *sacrament.*[1]

Personally, I like the word *sacrament.* Just try saying it out loud a few times. *Sac-ra-ment.* It's got that back-of-the-throat, conjuring-up-spit kind of sound. The first syllable rhymes with *smack,* as in "smack a tree trunk" or "smack your lips on fried chicken." It's a good solid word to convey the idea that God works through real stuff like trees and rocks, bread and wine, stars and human hands, to demonstrate his love for us.

Christians don't always agree on the exact number of the sacraments. The Protestant tradition has identified two special channels of

God's grace: baptism and the Lord's Supper. Other Christian traditions identify more, as many as seven. But even beyond our participation in formal sacraments of the church (which I believe is crucial for our growth as Christians), there are many ways to encounter God *sacramentally*. In other words, there are many ways in which God says, "I want you to know me, so come here: taste this bread, smell the incense, touch this tree, move your arms and dance with your whole body, drink the wine."

For instance, a friend told me this week that after living in China for many years, she was stunned to return to Long Island and see all the gorgeous trees. At one point in late autumn, she looked at a grove of trees, stripped of leaves and with their branches turned upward to the sky. She said it was as if the trees were raising their "hands" to God, singing with ardent praise and adoration. Is that just fanciful? Well then, what do we make of Psalm 96:12-13, which says, "Then all the trees of the forest will sing for joy; they will sing before the LORD, for he comes, he comes to judge the earth"? By observing that grove of trees, by joining their song of joy, my friend was praying sacramentally.

THE ENEMY OF SACRAMENTAL PRAYER

Some people view the concepts of sacraments and sacramental prayer with suspicion. "It's unsophisticated and unnecessary," they reply. "Why do I need trees and dirt and human hands and bread and wine to pray? After all, I'm a Christian. So if I can go straight to God with my brain and my words, why do I need this physical stuff?"

People are surprised to hear that these sentiments, in their extreme form, are actually connected with a strain of heresy lurking in the depths of anti-Christian, anti-biblical (and anti-Jewish) thought. The technical name for this heresy is Gnosticism. Ancient and contemporary Gnostics have at least one thing in common: a deep-seated mistrust of creation and matter and things and bodies. The "stuff" of the world is tainted, or at best irrelevant to their spiritual journey.

According to the brilliant contemporary theologian Hans Urs von Balthasar, "Always in the [early church's] background was the fundamental dogma of Gnosticism—the belief that the lower, material sphere, the 'flesh' . . . was contemptible, something to be vanquished, while the higher spiritual world was . . . the only thing worth cultivating."[2] Even bloody persecution posed less of a threat to the church than Gnosticism.[3]

But the early church rejected Gnosticism as radically sub-Christian because it denied a sacramental worldview. The sacramentally praying historical church has always fought with a fierce counterattack to Gnosticism: No, damn it (to borrow from C. S. Lewis),[4] the world God made is good. The things in this world are good. Human bodies are good. Yes, the world and things in the world are damaged and flawed, but they are worth fighting for and redeeming.

Throughout history the church has founded its sacramental exuberance on two great pillars of reality: creation and incarnation. A physical, sacramental way of praying begins on the very first page of your Bible: "God created the heavens and the earth. . . . God saw all that he had made, and it was very good" (Genesis 1:1, 31). Praying sacramentally begins with the goodness of creation. God delights in it all. And creation also matters because Christ is the one in whom and through whom "all things hold together" (Colossians 1:15-17).

The Chilean poet Pablo Neruda knew how to view creation sacramentally. Recently I spent time reading through his three volumes of odes to created things, poems in praise of ordinary items: an atom; a tuna; a glass of wine; a lizard; a woman gardening; and my personal favorite, the "Ode to a Lemon." After cutting a lemon in half, Neruda effused about the beauty of this "yellow goblet of miracles."[5]

Neruda was describing not a mere lemon but a miracle of creation. Much to my surprise, Neruda was a committed Marxist, but his poetry possesses a thoroughly biblical and sacramental bent. In classic Christian belief, God is separate from creation; but things, very particular things—lemons, oak leaves, rainbows, zebras, rivers, your neighbor's lungs, crickets, glaciers and your big toe—matter because God created the world, Jesus sustains the world, and the Spirit breathes new life into "the face of the earth" (Psalm 104:29-30).

The theology of sacramental prayer also rests on one more pillar: the incarnation. Jesus, the Son of God, entered the world of creation and became flesh. Thus, for the Christian, Jesus is the ultimate sacrament because he is the only one the Bible calls "the image of the invisible God" (Colossians 1:15). In other words, if you want to watch God, if you want to feel God, if you want to encounter God—look at Jesus. Jesus is God in stuff—skin, red blood cells, hair follicles, bladder and lungs and spleen.

Recently I met my friend Amy, who is not a follower of Christ, at a local Indian restaurant, where she grilled me with theological questions. Over *naan* and *tikka tikka masala* she ranted about "so-called Christians" who support a failed war in Iraq, rabidly advocate the death penalty, plunder the earth and then calmly consign non-Christians to eternal retribution. Finally, I interrupted her rant and said, "Amy, these are good questions, but if you really want to know about God, as a Christian I would say, look at Jesus. Read his life. Watch the way he interacted with outcasts and sinners and oppressors. Listen to his descriptions of truth and reality. According to the Bible, when you see the face of Jesus, you're watching God-in-action, God-in-human-flesh."

"No one has ever seen God," wrote the Gospel-writer John, "but God the One and Only, who is at the Father's side, has made him known" (John 1:18). Jesus is *the* sacrament of God.

This isn't just remote theology. If Gnosticism was the "first great temptation which Christian thought had to overcome,"[6] then the incarnation subdues and squashes its appeal. In contrast to a pale and vague Gnosticism, the incarnation ushers us into a colorful, creation-imbued path to the spiritual life. According to Hans Balthasar, "[Christianity] wholeheartedly acknowledged the goodness of creation and gladly and bravely affirmed man. . . . [T]he fact that God has become man, indeed flesh, proves that redemption and resurrection of the entire earthly world is not just a possibility but a reality."[7]

THE BIBLE'S SACRAMENTAL BENT

So why do we need the stuff of creation to help us connect with God?

The simple answer is this: because that's how God works. He set up his creation, and although it is fallen like us, it still declares his glory and goodness. God likes his creation, and God has chosen to work through it to "touch" us. It provides "handles" for us to know and to approach God. In the wise words of C. S. Lewis, "There is no good trying to be more spiritual than God. God never meant man to be a purely spiritual creature. That is why He uses material things like bread and wine to put the new life [of Jesus Christ] into us. We may think this rather crude and unspiritual. God does not: He invented eating. He likes matter. He invented it."[8]

I'm slowly discovering that there are hundreds of biblical examples of how God reaches out to us and we reach back through created stuff. For instance, after the Genesis flood, when God wanted to show his love for all of creation, he made a promise: "I now establish my covenant with you and with your descendants after you and with every living creature that was with you" (Genesis 9:9-10). But it wasn't just a verbal agreement; the covenant came with a physical sign—a rainbow. So God said, "This is the sign of the covenant I am making between me and you and every living creature with you, a covenant for all generations to come: I have set my rainbow in the clouds, and it will be the sign of the covenant between me and the earth" (Genesis 9:12-13). The rainbow became the "sacrament" of God's intent to preserve creation and maintain the covenant.

Years after Noah and the rainbow, God gave other signs of his covenant love to Abraham, starting with circumcision (see Genesis 17:10-11). Obviously a tattoo would have been much less invasive, but it's nearly impossible to ignore a circumcision. For the average guy, God's "sacramental touch" doesn't get more memorable than that. But notice that Abraham also had a lifelong sacramental relationship with God. At one point we read that God "took him outside and said, 'Look up at the heavens and count the stars—if indeed you can count them.' Then he said to him, 'So shall your offspring be'" (Genesis 15:5). I love that image of God taking Abraham by the hand, leading him outside his tent and pointing his gaze up to the night sky littered with stars. It was outside under the stars that God gave Abraham a clear picture of his promise.

Abraham also responded sacramentally to God. At one point we read that Abraham "planted a tamarisk tree in Beersheba, and there he called upon the name of the LORD, the Eternal God" (Genesis 21:33). Obviously he could have just "called upon the name of the LORD" without planting a tree. What's the point of planting a tree? The text doesn't say, but if we read it sacramentally, it's probable that the tree became a sign of Abraham's prayer life. Every time he saw the tree, he remembered God and his prayer.

The rest of the Old Testament is filled with sacramental reality. The Passover (see Exodus 12) became a sacramental experience. Even to this day, when our Jewish friends celebrate the Passover, they do it sacramentally: they taste and smell and feel and sing and touch. It's fascinating to note that God also experienced the Passover sacramentally: "The blood will be a sign for you," God said, "and *when I see the blood*, I will pass over you" (Exodus 12:13, emphasis added). Even God responds to the "sacrament," or sign, of the blood on the doorpost.

Worship inside the tabernacle was a full-bodied, fully sensual experience of sight and sound and smells. Finely twisted purple curtains (Exodus 26:1), the garments for the high priest (Exodus 28:2-3), the fragrant incense (Exodus 30:7), the aromatic spices—these things, these bodily experiences, declared the glory of God. And of course the Old Testament sacrificial system also engaged all of the senses. On the Day of Atonement (Leviticus 16), after slaughtering a bull and sprinkling its blood seven times on the atonement cover, after throwing incense on the fire and watching the smoke swirl and smelling the incense burn, after watching the priest place his hands on a live goat and confess everyone's sins over the goat's head, after sending the live goat into the desert, no one would leave the worship service muttering, "I just can't remember what the pastor preached on today."

The Psalms invite us to worship God with our bodies fully involved. God seems to tell us over and over again, "As you pray, don't just stand there; move your body. Shout, kneel, clap your hands, dance, bow down and even lie down. Just do something." God works and we respond to God sacramentally through the human body in motion.

One more example: when the apostle Paul wanted to pray for his young protégé in the faith, he didn't just use words; he reached out and touched him. So when Paul wanted to encourage Timothy to "fan into flame the gift of God," he told him that this gift "is in you *through the laying on of my hands*" (2 Timothy 1:6, emphasis added). Why did God work this way? Does God depend on human hands to impart his gifts to people? Well, yes and no. No, he doesn't have to do it that way; but yes, God often chooses to work sacramentally through our bodies and our actions. To paraphrase C. S. Lewis, God uses material things like hands to put the new life of Christ into us.

LIVING AND PRAYING SACRAMENTALLY (A MINIGUIDE FOR RECOVERING GNOSTICS)

Walking through these (and many more) passages has led me to two principles about a sacramental worldview. *First, in prayer we receive from God as he works through his creation to bless, reveal, redeem and love us.* The "sacrament" of the rainbow seems to set the stage for the rest of God's sacramental activity. When I ask people, "Who was the rainbow for?" they usually say, "Well, of course it was for us." But that's not what the story tells us. God said, "Whenever the rainbow appears in the clouds, I will see it and remember the everlasting covenant between God and all living creatures" (Genesis 9:16). In other words, the sacramental rainbow is primarily about God's activity, not ours. He acts through the sign. So praying sacramentally is primarily about receiving from the God who is acting on my behalf.

Also, *praying sacramentally involves our participation as we respond to God with faith through sacramentally charged actions:* planting a tree, raising our hands in prayer, viewing beautiful curtains in the tabernacle, gazing at stars or laying hands on someone as we pray.

But what difference does this make in our prayer life? How does this work its way into our lives? How do we pray sacramentally? How do I connect with God on a deeper level by this embodied way of praying? Based on my personal experience, let me share some sacramental practices that have made my prayer life come alive.

Begin with the Eucharist. In a truly biblical sacrament, we celebrate as a community centered around Jesus, the ultimate sacrament. Everything begins and feeds off the primal, sacramental experience of the Eucharist. Christians from different places and perspectives will never agree on the exact name—Eucharist, Lord's Supper, Holy Communion. Nor will we agree on exactly what happens during this sacrament. But based on our brief sacramental tour of the Bible, I contend that the Eucharist means two things: (1) God is at work through Jesus and in the power of the Holy Spirit to reveal, bless and redeem his people (and to draw others to a saving knowledge of himself as well). (2) We are responding to God's mystery of salvation in Christ by the sacramental acts of eating and drinking and sometimes kneeling and walking forward to receive the bread and the cup.

Every sacramental encounter with God flows from a Eucharistic life, that is, an intensely gospel-centered life. Surprisingly, many followers of Jesus seem to view the Lord's Supper as a glorified object lesson or children's sermon. A puny piece of bread and a tiny sip of wine (or grape juice) seem so simple and ordinary and childlike. In a way they are right: it is so simple and ordinary and childlike. But isn't that so like Jesus? He abolishes our Gnostic elitism and arrogance and creation revulsion. God destroys the notion that we have to find him in extraordinary places and in "spiritual" people who endure unending "spiritual quests" that lead to dead ends. God finds me and works within my life in ordinary places with ordinary people who belong to an ordinary community. Jesus is here, right now, in the ordinary stuff of life: bread and wine, this community of people, this pastor's flawed hands and words.

In a sense it does make me childlike, even beggarlike. As I come forward to receive the bread and the wine, I'm reminded that I'm joining a spiritual soup line. We're all famished for God and starving for grace, so we join the line of wasted, hungry, eager saints ready for our next meal from our Father. I need these physical, visible, tangible, tasty signs of God's grace to satisfy my hunger. As John Calvin said, "The sacraments, therefore, are exercises which make us more certain of the trustworthiness of God's Word. And because we are in flesh, they are shown under things of flesh to instruct us according to our dull capacity, and lead us by the hand as tutors lead children."[9] Or as a contemporary Catholic author put it, "I don't partake [of the Eucharist] because I'm a good Catholic, holy and pious and sleek. I partake because I'm a bad Catholic, riddled by doubt and anxiety and anger; fainting from severe hypoglycemia of the soul."[10]

God the Father initiates the relationship. Jesus invites us to the table of mercy. The Spirit descends on us. But living sacramentally in a sacramental universe also asks for our participation in the Lord's Supper. We do it as a community, but I can do my part to prepare and celebrate well. Do I truly acknowledge my hunger for God's grace? Am I open to receiving from Jesus at the Lord's Table? Do I prepare my heart the morning of or the night before celebrating the Lord's Supper? Do I view this as a holy time of true communion with the risen Jesus and with my fellow believers?

Everything flows from celebrating the Lord's Supper. In his battle against the Gnostics, the early church father Irenaeus summarized the centrality of the Lord's Supper: "Our teaching is consonant with what we do in the Eucharist, and the celebration of the Eucharist establishes what we teach."[11] Gnostic fantasies wither and die as we gather around the Lord's Table. Sacramental beauty blooms with life and colors and smells as we connect with the great Jesus-centered, gospel-grounded sacrament of the Eucharist.

Pray with other bodies. For far too long I tended to view my personal prayer life as my personal prayer life. I considered prayer a private transaction between me and God. By learning to pray sacramentally, I now see how much I need to pray with other bodies. I can develop my relationship with God by praying with you. Sacramental prayer has that hard-edged reality to it. You matter to my prayer life.

In the movie *Dead Man Walking* there is a powerful scene between

Sister Helen Prejean and a young man sentenced to die by lethal injection. Sister Helen tells him that when he's strapped in the chair, waiting to die, he should watch her face. "That way," she says, "the last thing you will see before you die will be the face of someone who loves you."[12]

Praying sacramentally means that I need to see your face as I pray. That's why part of my prayer life includes the spiritual discipline of praying with others. For me that means that I must meet with three other friends on a regular basis for two agenda items: (1) Sharing our lives, and (2) praying for each other. That's it. We don't try to study or solve problems. We take turns sharing our lives, and then we pray for each other. As I pray I need to see the face of these people who love me. Thus, sacramental prayer isn't about finding new ways to "jazz up" my prayer life; it's about finding my place in a specific, imperfect but beautiful-motley crew called the church of Jesus Christ.

Touch someone as you pray. Specifically, this concrete community is also a touch-based community. We touch as we pray, and we pray as we touch one another. I've noticed that Jesus was always touching people—children, lepers, blind men, sick women—and the apostle Paul touched Timothy and lit a fire in his heart (2 Timothy 1:6). In the early church, when someone was sick the elders were instructed to touch the sick person with oil and pray for him or her (James 5:14). It wasn't a suggestion; it was a commandment.

In a powerful scene from Ingmar Bergman's film *The Serpent's Egg*, a Catholic priest is taking off his vestments when a middle-aged woman enters the sacristy. Needy, lonely, insecure, she approaches the priest and begins to sob. She blurts out, "I'm so alone, Father, nobody loves me! God is so far away! I don't think he could love me anyway. Not the way I am! Everything is so dark for me!" At first the priest is just annoyed, but then he speaks tenderly to this woman: "Kneel down and I will bless you. God seems far away. He cannot touch you right now, I know that, but I am going to put my hands on your head and touch you—to let you know that you are not alone, not unlovable, not in the darkness. God is here and God does love you. When I touch you, God will touch you."[13]

I suppose we could argue, "What difference does it make whether I use oil or my hands or just speak the words? Does it really matter to you, God?" To which I imagine God saying, "Yes, it really matters. That's the way I like to work: through stuff. I like hands and olive oil. I invented both of them." Every time we touch someone as we pray we're eschewing Gnosticism and embracing a sacramental worldview.

Touch your community when you pray. Sacramental prayer, like every other path to prayer in this book, has an outward thrust of love on behalf of others. So praying sacramentally will propel us to ask, if Jesus is the Sacrament of God and if we are the body of Christ, then how are we "touching" our community with the touch of God? If my friend Amy is asking—even demanding—a sign of redemptive love from the church, then where are we providing those signs to others around us? A true, full-bodied, sacramentally praying follower of Jesus will want to be close enough and engaged enough to see the faces of those who don't know Jesus. We are the sacrament of God's presence for our local community.

Go outside when you pray. Sometimes improving your connection with God is that simple: go outside when you pray. Lately I've been struck by how much of the Bible's storyline occurs outdoors. The Kentucky farmer-essayist Wendell Berry once commented, "The great visionary encounters [of the Bible] did not take place in temples, but in sheep pastures, in the desert, in the wilderness, on mountains, on the shores of rivers and sea. . . . I don't think it's enough appreciated how much an outdoor book the Bible is. . . . It is best read and understood outdoors, and the further outdoors the better. . . . Passages that within walls seem improbable or incredible, outdoors seem merely natural. This is because outdoors we are confronted everywhere with wonders; we see that the miraculous is not extraordinary but the common mode of existence. It is our daily bread."[14]

He's right. Creation, the exodus, the reception of the Ten Commandments, the conquest of the Promised Land, the birth and ministry of Jesus, the preaching ministry of Jesus, the crucifixion and resurrection of Jesus, the daring deeds of the early church and the missionary travels of Paul—most of the important events in the Bible occurred outside.

So go outside. Read a portion of the Bible, go for a long walk in the woods, and talk to God about what you just read. I have a special place in a bird sanctuary under an apple tree where I sit on a hard wooden bench every morning from early spring to late fall. So with the steam from my hot coffee swirling, I sit under the apple tree listening to bird songs, watching the sun rise, smelling the grass and flowers, reading my Bible and listening to God. My five senses are wide open as creation "declare[s] the glory of God" (Psalm 19:1). By praying outside, immersed in apples and hard wood and songbirds, I am beginning to pray as a true sacramentalist.

Move your body when you pray. This idea is ancient and very simple: read the Psalms and then go and do likewise. So when the psalmist writes, "Let us kneel before the Lord our Maker" (Psalm 95:6), we kneel as we pray. When the psalmist says, "Let us shout aloud to the Rock of our salvation" (Psalm 95:1), we really shout. When the psalmist prays by raising his hands before God (Psalm 63:4), we practice raising our hands in prayer.

I've often excused myself from such demonstrative behavior by appealing to my upbringing and ethnicity. Obviously, I don't need to move my body like everyone else, but I also must allow for the possibility that I'm more comfortable praying like a Gnostic. Sacramental prayer is embodied prayer. The bodily actions do make a difference; the actions and gestures may even become a prayer. Let's say someone stuck a gun in your back and said, "I have a gun; I'm pressing it into your flesh, so do not turn around. Just raise your hands slowly, and I'll take your wallet." You'd probably raise your hands because your hand raising would send an embodied message: "I hear you and I am surrendering to your wishes." The physical action speaks louder than words. In the same way, when we pray sacramentally—with shouting, kneeling, hand raising, bowing down, falling on our faces, even just standing or closing our eyes versus opening our eyes—our bodies become a prayer offering to God.

The early church recognized the importance of bodily actions and gestures when they described the beauty of praying by making the sign of the cross. "In all our travels and movements," wrote Tertullian in A.D. 204, "in all our comings in and going out, in putting on our shoes, at the bath, at the table, in lighting of candles, in lying down, in sitting down, whatever employment occupies us, we mark our foreheads with the sign of the cross."[15] Making the sign of the cross on our forehead or on our body isn't a meaningless gesture; it's a prayer in itself, a prayer-in-motion.

Of course, making the sign of the cross is only one example of moving your body as you pray. I love taking my beagle for a walk late at night. While my beagle tugs and pants, I walk and pray. Sometimes I don't say much to God; I just listen. But the very act of moving, walking, looking up into the stars, opens up my brain and body and soul to the presence of God. If you're not that physically inclined, even the simple act of sitting with your palms upraised is an embodied way to tell God, "I'm open. Fill me, Lord."

Or if you really want to immerse yourself in sacramental reality, make something with your own hands. Two years ago I found a marvelous recipe for mulligatawny, a savory soup that combines butter, chicken, carrots, turnips, lentils, golden raisins, curry, cloves and cracked pepper. The taste and aroma are stunning. Every time I slice the turnips, crack the peppers, and smell the combination of curry and cloves, I'm reminded why I'm not a Gnostic. I like creation. I want to stick my nose and immerse my taste buds into the goodness of creation.

So as a sacramentally praying Christ-follower, I'll continue praying with my eyes wide open. I'll immerse my life in the hard, prickly, smelly, sticky, bumpy, dirty, tasty stuff of creation. However, praying sacramentally isn't so much about what we do (i.e., follow these six steps and perk up your prayer life) but about how we live. The world drips with the rich, gooey honey of sacramental reality. God made it that way. God likes it that way. So go ahead and bake some bread. Cut wood and make a bookshelf. Plant some squash or petunias. Draw a picture. Play the flute or guitar. Honestly, it will help your prayer life. God loves his creation. We just have to taste it, smell it, touch it, see it and move with it. It's the way God made you, and he likes it that way.

3

PRAYER AS DESPERATION

On a bright and calm summer afternoon I was casually eating a sandwich on a park bench with my friend Kevin. After discussing weighty intellectual topics, Kevin suddenly asked me about a friend of mine named Doc, a man who had been my mentor and main encourager for over a decade. I paused and said quietly, "You know, it's been eight years since Doc died." "What do you miss the most about him?" Kevin asked. Much to my surprise, with a lump in my chest I blurted out, "I need someone to tell me I'm doing okay in life."

I tried to take the words back, but two in particular hung in the air: *"I need."* I said the words with such force and simplicity that they stunned me. I tried to backtrack, editing my response, giving it a more upbeat and "spiritual" spin, but it was too late. And then I wondered, why was I so embarrassed? What is it about saying *"I need"* that makes me cringe with shame?

I don't like admitting my needs, and I certainly don't want others to consider me a needy human being. I'd rather say, "I'll give" or "I'm in charge" or "I'm okay" or "I can." But "I need" sounds so utterly human: dependent, vulnerable and at times even downright desperate. I'd rather ban those two words from my conversations and work feverishly to prove that I'm far from desperation.

CRYING OUT TO GOD: PRAYER AS HUMAN NEED

Unfortunately, my aversion to "I need" thwarts my relationship with God because on one level prayer is rooted in need. One of the most common biblical words to describe how humans communicate with God is the word *cry* or the phrase *cry out*. It's never an insipid, calm cry, as in "Uh, God, if you're not too busy and you're coming by anyway, would you mind giving me a little boost?" *Cry* and *cry out* always imply urgency, neediness and even desperation. In the Old Testament the Hebrew words for *cry* literally mean "to shriek" *(zawak)*, "to holler" *(shawvah)* and "to creak or make a shrill sound" *(rinnaw)*. In the New Testament the primary Greek word for crying out *(kradzo)* means "to croak like a raven" or "to scream."

Exodus 2:23 contains the first time "cry out" is used in the Bible to describe our relationship with God: "The Israelites groaned in their slavery and cried out, and their cry for help because of their slavery went up to God." In the next chapter of Exodus we find a God who responds to our cries by saying, "I have indeed seen the misery of my people in Egypt. I have heard them *crying out*. . . . And now the *cry* of the Israelites has reached me" (Exodus 3:7, 9, emphasis added).

From that point in the biblical story, the practice of crying out to God becomes habitual. Someone is always crying out to God. The Psalms—the ancient prayer book of the Bible—are filled with people in trouble who cry out to God:

> "I waited patiently for the LORD; he turned to me and heard my cry." (Psalm 40:1)
>
> "I cry out to God Most High, to God, who fulfills his purpose for me." (Psalm 57:2)
>
> "I call on the LORD in my distress, and he answers me." (Psalm 120:1)
>
> "Out of the depths I cry to you, O LORD; O Lord, hear my voice. Let your ears be attentive to my cry for mercy." (Psalm 130:1-2)
>
> "I cry aloud to the LORD; I lift up my voice to the LORD for mercy.

I pour out my complaint before him; before him I tell my trouble." (Psalm 142:1-2)

"O LORD, hear my prayer, listen to my cry for mercy; in your faithfulness and righteousness come to my relief." (Psalm 143:1)

So we can draw some conclusions about prayer: (1) Prayer isn't always neat or pretty—sometimes it's very messy; (2) prayer isn't always quiet—sometimes it's very loud; (3) prayer isn't always calm—sometimes it's very passionate. Prayer involves coming to God in the mess of life, the confusion of life, the pain and agony of life, and crying out for help. Prayer begins with these words: *God, help! God, I (or we) need you!* God designed prayer for desperate human beings.

This should be a relief because we often assume that prayer requires a long series of prerequisites: Get in the right mood. Find the right place. Compose the correct words. Conjure up the right feelings. Banish distractions. Rid your life of ugly emotions like hate and anger and lust. But in the biblical story the first rule about prayer or crying out to God is that "prayer begins where we are, not where we think we should be." In his book titled *The Art of Prayer,* my friend Tim Jones quotes this rule and then claims that "no conviction has done more to free me to turn to God. . . . God wants *me.* I do not need to put on airs to try to give myself a spiritual makeover to talk with God."[1]

I've experienced this on a human level. When my daughter was two years old, she was the messiest eater I've ever seen. She would smear everything—spaghetti sauce, chocolate pudding, strained beets and squash—all over her hands, feet and face, and then for her grand finale she'd take the bowl and dump it on her head. Covered with a slobbery mess of sauce and grease and sugar, she'd lift her arms to me and say, "Help, Daddy! Out of chair, please!"

That's how we come to our heavenly Father. In Christ, because of Christ, through Christ, we come to God the Father just as we are. Prayer implies freedom: not the freedom to sin, of course, but the freedom to live as children of God; the freedom to stand in Christ's righteousness; the freedom that comes from the Holy Spirit, who urges us to cry out, "*Abba,* Father" (Galatians 4:6, emphasis in original). Prayer is not just "saying prayers"; it's being with our heavenly Father, crying out to him from the depth of our need.

TROUBLE IS NEAR

Of course, our neediness also implies an unpleasant reality about being human: it's called trouble. Psalm 22:11 succinctly reminds us that "trouble is near." That's what it means to journey through this fallen and broken planet with deeply flawed people: trouble is near. No matter how long we live or how much we try to avoid it, like a thug in a back alley, trouble is always waiting for us. The great Polish writer Isaac Bashevis Singer once said, "I only pray when I'm in trouble, but I'm always in trouble, so I'm always praying."

Sometimes people ask me, "So, how are you doing? Are you staying out of trouble?" Just once I'd like to say something like this:

> What kind of question is that? Are you kidding? I'm *always* in trouble. I'm a flawed human being trying to raise four children. I'm trying to love well—my wife, my friends, my enemies, the poor—but I have a reservoir of selfishness inside my heart. Yes, I'm in trouble! I'm trying to listen to "God's still, small voice" but there are so many other voices and distractions that hook into my mouth and jerk me around. I'm an addict to my favorite sins. And not only that, but I believe that God is holy and just and that by myself I stand under his condemnation. Based on my track record, I'm lost and accursed. Am I in trouble? You tell me. In the years ahead I will face suffering, trials, misunderstandings, grief and loss. We're all in trouble. The Bible says that we're up to our necks in an intense spiritual battle, wrestling "not against flesh and blood, but against . . . the powers of this dark world and against the spiritual forces of evil" (Ephesians 6:12). We're no match for this. And then we have another enemy—death—and every day we're getting a little closer to its poisonous "sting." So all in all, in answer to your question, no, I'm not staying out of trouble.

Although I've never actually delivered this rant, it reminds me that prayer begins and continues with the reality that trouble will stay near until the day I die. I can't fight the trouble on my own. I have wits and resources and a human will, but in many of these battles I'm seriously overmatched—no, I'm completely helpless. But that fact actually makes my prayer life come alive. As Tim Jones contends, "Prayer borne of need can teach us humble dependence. I wonder if God may allow us to meet times of profound need because he knows that they have potential to turn us toward him. Not that he inflicts pain, but he knows how in difficult times we are less likely to believe the myth that our ingenuity and self-sufficiency are adequate."[2]

Of course, here's the amazing good news: when we unabashedly admit our need, when we cry out to God from the depths of our helplessness, God hears our cry. When we cry out, God pays attention. Exodus 2:23-24 describes God's response to his people's trouble: "and their cry for help . . . went up to God. God heard their groaning." God hears the cry of the needy (see Job 34:28). God responds to those who cry out to him, because he is compassionate (see Exodus 22:27). Clearly God is moved by our need and our trouble. Our cry pierces God's heart.

Prayer is God's great invitation to come to him in the midst of our trouble and receive God's resources. "Call to me," God urges us, "and I will answer you and tell you great and unsearchable things you do not know" (Jeremiah 33:3). God is abounding in love and power. God issues the invitation. All of this seems so simple, doesn't it? It's a simple, precise, tidy, three-point outline:

God is good and rich with resources.
We're in trouble.
God invites us to come and receive help.

How hard is that? We just need to connect three dots. We should rise up, jump into God's arms and declare, "Yes, I'll come. Yes, I'll ask. Yes, I'm here with my hands open wide like a giant basket to receive hope from you, Father." So what's the problem? Why is prayer so difficult? Why don't we come?

Identifying Our Greatest Prayer Barriers

It seems to me that we have two huge barriers to our prayer life, both of which are rooted in our sinful nature. First, we're proud. We don't ask because admitting our need and asking for help makes us look incompetent, incomplete, broken and flawed—and our pride resents appearing needy. So pride whispers, "You're not that bad. *Desperation*—my, my, what a strong and repulsive word! You may face a few minor 'troubles'—sin, eternal damnation, demonic powers, addictive cycles, death, suffering, entrenched selfishness—but, not to worry, you can conquer them."

I must confess that at least part of me cringes as I write this chapter. What if a sophisticated and intellectual reader picks up my book and starts with this chapter? Will they scoff at my description of desperation? Will they assume that Christians really are backwards anti-intellectuals? Of course, these fears merely reveal the pride festering in the damp corners of my heart.

But I'm not only proud; I'm also deeply insecure. Insecurity intercepts us on our path to God, grabs us by the throat and hisses, "Wait a minute, who are you to approach God and ask for what you need? The universe is a vast place, and you're a mere speck—sometimes a dirty speck—on a crumb of a planet. If God is really there, why would God care about you?" After my friend Betsy lost her husband to cancer, she told me, "I feel so completely and eternally unlovable. My husband 'abandoned' me. I know it wasn't his fault, but I feel so alone now. Why would anyone—including God—ever want to love me?"

Of course, we do have some solid reasons to feel insecure. When Blaise Pascal, the devout fifteenth-century mathematician, pondered the immensity of the cosmos (he called it the nothingness from which we emerge and the infinity which engulfs us), and our specklike existence in it, he declared with a shudder, "I am moved to terror. . . . The eternal silence of these infinite spaces fills me with dread."[3] We really are specks on a speck of a planet.

But on the other hand, the gospel proclaims news that should stun us with its utter beauty: Jesus has reconciled us to God the Father, so in Christ, through Christ, with Christ, on behalf of Christ, who died for our sins, who rose again and who intercedes for us, we can bury our pride and insecurity forever. Christ paid the debt for our sin. Jesus removed the list of charges against us (see Colossians 2:13-15). In him we receive his perfect record of righteousness, and he gives it to us only by grace as a free gift from God. So the Bible tells us, "In him [Christ] and through faith in him we may approach God with *freedom* and *confidence*" (Ephesians 3:12, emphasis added). Jesus replaces our pride and insecurity with a glorious new way to come to the Father—with freedom and confidence.

THE STORY OF A DESPERATE MAN

That's why I love the story of the desperate man named Bartimaeus (see Mark 10:46-52). In the presence of Jesus, Bartimaeus exudes freedom and confidence. Notice his lack of pride. He's a mess: blind, ragged, poor. He's begging for every scrap he can get. He's desperate and not afraid to admit it. He heard that Jesus was passing by, so without a shred of propriety, he started shouting, "Jesus, Son of David, have mercy on me!" (Mark 10:47). The people around Jesus (i.e., the disciples) are trying hard not to be desperate people. They are the "decent" people—the untroubled, unfazed, righteous and very cool followers of Jesus. Typically, desperate people repulse decent people. So in this Gospel story the decent people tell Bartimaeus to shut up and go away ("Many rebuked him" [Mark 10:48]).

Like the people in the crowd around Bartimaeus, decent people (like me!) often excel at two things: busyness and bossiness. So they bustle around Bartimaeus, giving advice, authoritatively instructing and guiding him. Like most of us, they are trying to be helpful. And notice how helpful they are! They shield Jesus from the annoying, smelly, but very scrappy desperate man. *Helpfulness* always puts us in control; *helplessness* makes us relinquish control and cry out to God like Bartimaeus. Of course, the crowd's "helpfulness" doesn't faze Bartimaeus. He spurns their shallow religious piety, crying out *(kradzo)* even louder, "Son of David, have mercy on me!"

In verse 49 we read that "Jesus stopped." This is amazing. Back in verse 32 we find that "they [Jesus and his disciples] were on their way to Jerusalem, with Jesus leading the way." It's an intense scene: Jesus is on a quest to charge into Jerusalem so he can die for the sins of the world and rise again to bring new life to all of creation. He's on a colossal, world-transforming assignment. With fire in his eyes and passion in his gut, Jesus leads the way. Jesus will not be stopped. When his strongest disciple, Simon Peter, tries to interrupt Jesus' mission, Jesus tells him, "Get behind me, Satan!" (Mark 8:33).

But then, suddenly, something makes him stop. Someone is crying out to God. Some desperate beggar shrugs off all the naysayers and the decent, respectable people who pray with calm, cool precision, and he actually dares to cry out to God. In the presence of Jesus, he doesn't have a crumb of insecurity. He experiences total freedom and confidence. So when Jesus asks, "What do you want me to do for you?" he simply says, "I want to see." Bartimaeus cries out—boldly, confidently, without hemming and hawing or apologizing. He excels at exuberant, confident and hope-charged desperation.

Bartimaeus understood the essence of prayer: prayer is an incredible invitation from a generous God for people in need. A good and holy God, who is our Father through Christ, invites us to come. We're in trouble. We need help, and we cry out, "God, help. I need you. We need you." And then God says, "It's about time! It's about time you banished the illusion of your independence, your pride and your insecurity. You were born a needy human being; you will die a needy human being; and between those two great bookmarks of birth and death, you will live as a needy human being. The secret is out: you need. Like Bartimaeus, you are a desperate human being. But I am also generous. So come, ask, call to me and cry out."

THE FRUIT OF DESPERATION

I've come to embrace prayer as desperation through a long, slow, painful process. Okay, I came to it kicking and screaming. My parents and teachers and coaches and even my churches didn't raise me to be *des-*

perate. They encouraged me to be a decent, unneedy, nondesperate human being. I can still remember my tryouts for Little League baseball as a ten-year-old boy. I possessed average abilities, but I was tall and fairly coordinated. So for tryouts my dad told me to wear a thick red sweatshirt because it would make me look older and tougher. It worked. I was one of the few ten-year-olds who made the "majors" of Little League. I made the team and learned a profound lesson: you only make it in life by acting good, competent, tough and perfect.

So it's no wonder that the message of "look good, look competent, act tough" lodged deep in my heart. It's not an entirely false message. Obviously, I'm not totally incompetent at everything. I'm not *desperate* when it comes to writing a paragraph, balancing the checkbook, buying a new suit, raking my lawn, making money and a whole host of things. But I am desperate when it comes to growing in love, nurturing hope, standing for justice, battling sin and Satan, conquering death, creating life-giving communities, and overcoming my addictions (to name a few). So when competence and perfection become the primary messages in our hearts, we begin to resent our weakness and neediness. Sometimes I even hear people (including myself) say, "I can't get sick right now. I'm too busy to be needy." Underneath it all, the message rings clear: "Neediness is utterly abnormal. It's unfair to be needy and desperate. I resent it and rail against it."

I'm slowly learning the gospel truth about crying out to God: embracing our weakness and then crying out to God unleashes God's power and mercy. Again, God drew me to this conclusion as I kicked and screamed against him. But as I read through the Bible, over and over (and over and over) again, I saw a clear pattern develop: When we don't admit our need, we're headed for disaster. When we hit bottom and embrace our desperation and then cry out to God, God's power and mercy are quickly unleashed in us and through us.

Specifically, I've noticed that when God's people understand prayer as desperation, it radically transforms our worship. When we're actively crying out to God, we're also open and hungry before God. We're expectant, thirsty, empty-handed people who come ready to receive. As an older African American prayer says, "O Lord, we come this morning knee-bowed and body-bent before Thy throne of grace . . . like empty pitchers to a full fountain."[4] But when we all come to God like empty pitchers, it energizes our corporate praise and worship. We know we need God. We're all desperate human beings, but we're also desperate human beings who are crying out to God, waiting on God, following hard after God, being passionately pursued by God, open and ready to get filled with God's glory.

We're not gathering as "the audience." Nor do we come to analyze or critique the services. Instead, we enter worship with a history of desperation. We've been the empty pitcher—dry, dusty, cracked and desperate. And we've also been filled with the "full fountain" of God's mercy. We've come to God's throne of grace "knee-bowed and body-bent," but we've also left with our backs straightened, our heads held high and our shackled hearts unleashed by God's power. God delighted in us, and we delighted in God. As a result, as desperate but delighted human beings, we always have a story to share and a song to sing. When we gather together for worship, our story of desperation and God's graces gets unleashed in us and out through us.

I've also noticed that our corporate desperation deepens and enriches our experience of Christian community. Communities remain inauthentic and false when we never dare to cry out to God in the presence of our brothers and sisters. Instead, week after tedious week, we piously assemble for our small groups or committee meetings and worship services, but none of us exhibit desperation. Amazingly, Jesus has delivered every one among us from every need. Yes, it's astounding but true: our neediness has been abolished, our desperation fully healed!

Unfortunately, nondesperate Christian community isn't a happy place. People rarely laugh or cry or hug or love. They just repeat stale clichés that no one actually believes. Any community that attempts to sanitize itself from desperation eventually starts to reek with a decayed, musty boredom. And it's boring because everyone knows that the entire community is trapped in a lie, the colossal lie called "I'm okay."

There's nothing as stale as a nondesperate Christian community.

Crying out to God makes authentic community come alive. Desperation is usually the last thing we want to stick on our tightly controlled agendas, but when I admit my desperation and you admit yours, when we lean hard into God, when we cry out to him from our places of trouble, suddenly community comes alive. It's charged with reality. I need you, you need me, and together we need the living God, so we cry out for mercy.

I'll never forget my first taste of desperate community. I would wake up at 4:00 every Tuesday morning and drive two hours to meet with eight men and our leader, Paul. By the time I arrived, I was dying for the fresh coffee and bagels, but I didn't come for the food. I came for the honesty, the reality, the deep sense that we were all desperate, thirsty, hungry men. We craved God, and we craved our friendships. Like the broken bread for Communion, our lives were broken open to one another. Paul always gently led us into the healing presence of Jesus, but it was a community journey, not a solo journey. Desperation opens my life to other believers in a rich depth of authenticity.

Of course, this leads to one more beautiful fruit of desperation: we become a compassionate community that reaches out to a broken world. True prayer isn't mere private piety; it changes us, and it changes the world around us. As a community, when we learn to cry out to God, it trains our hearts and ears to listen for the outcries around us. Desperate, messy, ragged people (the Bartimaeus people of the world) no longer shock us or repulse us because we are the desperate people (perhaps we could call our churches "Desperation-R-Us"). We know what it's like to be in need. We know how to cry out for help. We're experts on human weakness—our own weakness, that is. And as a result, God softens our heart toward others. We develop compassion, and we listen for the cries of struggle and desperation that most of the world ignores.

Jewish author James Kugel observed that in the Hebrew Bible the word for "cry out" doesn't refer to mere praying. There are many other fine Hebrew words to describe prayer in general. Kugel claims that the Hebrew word for "cry out" was often used as shorthand for the cry of the victimized, the helpless or the oppressed members of society. Thus, God promises that when widows or orphans are oppressed and they cry out to him, he will become angry and kill with the sword (Exodus 22:22-24). If someone deprives a poor man of his own garment and he cries out to God, God says, "I will hear, for I am compassionate" (Exodus 22:27). So Kugel concludes: "It is the oppressed human's cry . . . that will unleash the chain of events that will ultimately result in your being punished. I am powerless not to react, God seems to say, once the abused party cries out to me."[5]

So prayer doesn't just help us face our own trouble; it tunes us to the troubles of others around us, especially the poor, the abused, the oppressed and those who have been or are being victimized by the powerful. God hears these cries for help. As we pray, we learn to pay attention to this quiet suffering as well.

My friend Saul loves to tell the story that propelled him to his ministry with the poorest of the poor in Mexico City. Although he grew up in Mexico, he had never seen the desperate poverty on the edge of the city. But one calm Sunday afternoon, an acquaintance drove him up a winding hill that overlooked a massive dump. This enormous, human-made crater contained tons of garbage. A dark brown river of raw sewage gurgled through the piles of garbage. As he gazed into the bottom of the pit, Saul realized that there were actually people scurrying around on the steep slopes that dropped into the dump. By scavenging for food and scraps of junk to sell, they tried to eke out a living in the shacks built on the edge of the dump.

Initially Saul was stunned and outraged. He muttered, "Human beings should not live like this! This is a crime, and something must be done." As he turned from staring into the dump, still fuming and muttering, he noticed a small boy only a few yards away. The boy was digging into a mound of garbage at the top of the hill that descended into the dump. After a frantic search, the boy pulled out a few scraps of a wilted, dirt-covered orange peel, sat down on the pile of garbage and proceeded to devour his "meal." Saul's heart broke with compassion. For the next twenty years (and still going) Saul and his wife, Pilar, would dedicate their lives to working among the desperately poor and hungry in Mexico City and Oaxaca.

Prayer as desperation does that to us. It changes our hearts. It trains us to see, to smell, to hear the undecent, broken, poor, crying-out people around us. We can't ignore them anymore. We can't hide from them anymore. We can't banish them anymore. For the God and Father of our Lord Jesus Christ hears the cries of the afflicted and the desperate. If we come to him, he will hear our cries. And if we keep coming to him, he will tune our ears to the cries of the world around us.

PRACTICING DESPERATION

"Practicing desperation." That phrase still jars me, but it sums up a major feature of my current prayer life. I'm slowly learning that desperation is a continuous human state that leads me to cry out to God habitually, without shame or regret.

I wanted to close this chapter with a big, "dramatic" story of God's intervention in the midst of my trouble and desperation. But it's much more honest to share something modest, small and ordinary. Lately most of my prayer life consists of a simple practice: late at night, while everyone in the house is sleeping, I light a single, long white candle to remind me of the presence of the risen Christ. Then I fall to my knees, raise my arms toward God and quietly repeat something like "Abba, Father" or "Lord Jesus, have mercy on me, a sinner." Then the words tumble out: "I'm in trouble because . . . I need you because . . ." I ask for what I need. It's a given that every day I need at least four qualities: wisdom, courage, love and patience. I never have enough of those qualities, and I usually need to ask for mercy because I didn't have them.

And then I ask on behalf of others. For example, "Lord Jesus, Joe is fighting a battle tonight, and he's crying out to you. Catherine is in the hospital; she's ninety-one and she's so alone and frightened. Help her, God. So many are hungry tonight, Father. They're in trouble and need food. Help them, God."

After listing the specific things that trouble me and others, I sit in the near darkness and listen for God's word of love. Actually, the more I know myself, the utterly desperate human being that I am, the more likely I am to cry out to God. And the more I know God, the stunningly good and generous God and Father of Jesus, the more likely I am to cry out to him.

All in all, prayer isn't really that difficult. It all starts with crying out to God. And our God cannot help but respond to the exuberant, confident and hope-charged prayer of desperation.

4

PRAYER AS MYSTERY

I was driving my daughter from Long Island, New York, to Wheaton, Illinois, when our Suburban suddenly started dying on the freeway. Our cell phone didn't work and it was 7:30 in the morning, so I said a quiet, short prayer to God. I *happened* to be right by an exit, so we headed into Blakeslee, Pennsylvania. We coasted down a hill until our car *happened* to die right in front of the local police station. The police dispatcher said, "Oh, are you ever in luck. Jimmy the tow truck guy just *happened* to call and say that he's right around corner." Jimmy came within three minutes, picked us up, towed us to his shop and even dropped us off for breakfast (which just *happened* to be at Blakeslee's own "Chat 'N' Chew" Restaurant). Jimmy just *happened* to have a cancellation, so he got us into the shop immediately. It just *happened* to be a loose connection on the battery, so we pulled back onto I-90 in one hour. We praised God for the power of prayer. It was as smooth and quick as buttering toast.

Compare that story with another story: My friend Susan was struggling with depression. Lonely and confused, she wandered on one of our Long Island beaches, pouring her heart out to God. "God, just give me a sign—one sign!—that you are really there." As she prayed, a lovely, lone seagull began circling over her head. "Could this be the sign of your goodness, Lord?" she wondered. She watched the beautiful bird floating gently in the sky, and she stood frozen on the beach as the seagull emitted a blob of grey, slimy seagull doo-doo. The grey glob plummeted from the sky and landed right on her head. Touché! At the time, she felt God say, "Here's your answer: *splat!*"

THE PROBLEM DEFINED

The mystery behind these two scenarios is clear: Why does God seem to answer some prayers in a quick, tidy, even miraculous fashion but then other prayers—which are just as sincere, God-honoring and faith-inspired—seem to hit the ceiling and bounce back? As a pastor and a follower of Jesus, I've struggled with the reality of this second scenario. We pray, we cry out, we trust Jesus for great things and reasonable and God-honoring things, we pray boldly and passionately, and then zilch, nada, silence. Or maybe things even get worse. Some people pray for healing, and a loved one dies. Others pray for God to save a marriage, and then the divorce papers come anyway. Many of my friends ask God to remove temptation—the lure of lust or the craving for alcohol or persistent rage and bitterness—and the enticement to sin grows stronger. Throughout the years, I've noticed that most of us don't want to talk about this problem. I seldom hear people attending small groups and telling their friends, "Hey, I have another unanswered prayer I'd like to share." But it seems like everyone has one, two or an entire bagful of unanswered prayers.

And then the Bible seems to increase the tension. Jesus himself made some astounding promises about answered prayer: "Whatever you ask for in prayer, believe that you have received it, and it will be yours" (Mark 11:24). And he said, "You may ask me for anything in my name, and I will do it" (John 14:14). Those promises seem clear: ask and you'll get what you ask for.

As I said in chapter three ("Prayer as Desperation"), we should come expectantly and pray boldly with freedom and confidence (see Ephesians 3:12). We should ask God for great things (see Jeremiah 33:3). But what if we come and pray boldly and expectantly, and we don't receive answers, or at least the answers we expected?

Surprisingly, I've noticed that rather than avoiding the messy problem of unanswered prayer, the Bible delves into it with remarkable candor. It admits the problem and then even gives concrete examples of this painful reality. I've never heard anyone provide a neat, unified theory that explains every instance of unanswered prayer. On the other hand, at the very least I can explore some of the unanswered prayers found right on the pages of God's Word. After you explore these case studies of unanswered prayers, I hope you can draw your own conclusions and construct your own theories about the mystery of God and the mystery of prayer.

HONESTLY STRUGGLING WITH THE MYSTERY

My friend Jill, a brilliant Ph.D. student in engineering and a heartfelt follower of Christ, kept praying for two things: she asked God to heal her depression and to give her a husband. From Jill's perspective, God did not answer those prayers, so she ditched God. I've always wondered if I could have said something more helpful. It's not as simple as it sounds. Her depression stemmed from profound issues of abuse and abandonment; she was raped and terrorized as a child. And the request for a husband also seemed reasonable to me. I, too, prayed that God would give her a husband. But Jill grew weary of the pain, so she told me, "I've had it. I just turned thirty-five, and God hasn't come through for me, so I'm packing up my Bible and my prayer journal and I'm saying goodbye to God. Wouldn't it just be easier to *not* believe in God? Believing in God just sets me up for deep disappointment, and I've had enough disappointment in my life."

On one level her prayer requests may seem self-centered; but on another level Jill's anguish was real. How do we unravel the mystery of unanswered prayer for Jill? Surprisingly, I've discovered that the Bible doesn't always begin with "answers"; instead, sometimes God asks us to enter the struggle and the question of unanswered prayer.

In this regard, the book of Psalms, the foundational guide to prayer, serves as an invaluable resource for identifying and expressing our confusion. Nearly one-third of the 150 Psalms contain elements of lament, brutally honest cries to God from places of abandonment. Laments are an invitation to come before God and the community of God's people so we can express the pain of unanswered prayer. They aren't happy prayers; laments usher us into a world of hurt and anger and darkness.

At times these prayers of lament grow dark, but none of them are as dark as Psalm 88. It begins with a smidgen of hope: "O LORD, the God who saves me, day and night I cry out before you." But the psalmist is in trouble, and God doesn't seem to help: "For my soul is full of trouble. . . . You have put me in the lowest pit, in the darkest depths. . . . I am confined and cannot escape; my eyes are dim with grief" (Psalm 88:3, 6, 8-9). In other words, he prays, "God, you don't help; you just drop bird poop on my head."

Every other psalm of lament eventually returns to hope and trust in God. The psalmist cries out to God in his pain; he even yells and argues with God. But then the prayer softens as he calmly proclaims, "But I still trust in you, God." Psalm 88 is the exception to that pattern. In this prayer the psalmist cries out to God; he's sincere; he believes the right things about God—but help doesn't seem to come. The final verse says, "You have taken my companions and loved ones from me; the darkness is my closest friend." This prayer trails off in unresolved tension, doubt, hurt, anguish and mystery.

If you're like me, on most days I'd prefer to slice Psalm 88 out of the Bible. If Thomas Jefferson could surgically remove 90 percent of the four Gospel accounts, why not take out one psalm? Psalm 88 isn't upbeat. It doesn't end like a typical American sitcom with the happy music starting as the family hugs and everything gets resolved. As Kathleen Norris contends, "All-American optimism, largely a middle-class Protestant phenomenon, doesn't want to know this world. We want to conquer evil by being nice, and nice people don't soil their white gloves with the gritty anger at the heart of a cursing [or a lament] psalm."[1]

But Christians believe that the Bible is God's Holy Spirit–inspired Word. So Psalm 88 is God's dark, messy, painful gift to us. As Norris says, "You come to the [Psalms] through all the moods and conditions of life, and while you may feel like hell, you sing it anyway. To your surprise, you find that the psalms do not deny your true feelings but allow you to reflect on them, right in front of God and everyone else."[2]

In my thirty years as a follower of Jesus, I've heard bright, positive "Christian talk" that tries to simplify and classify the mystery of unanswered prayer. The typical outline goes like this: God always answers prayer; sometimes he says yes, sometimes he says no, and sometimes he says wait. The outline isn't false; it's just trivial. It doesn't honor suffering. I don't want my anguish to fit into "point one" or "point two" in a sermon outline. It polishes the ragged edge off mystery, making it smooth and happy, but it leaves me cold and empty.

I've also heard Christians say that our prayers remain unanswered because we did something wrong. We didn't follow the formula or have enough faith. Certainly there can be something amiss in our prayers, but that doesn't explain everything. I don't see any bad theology or spirituality in Psalm 88. The renowned scientist-theologian John Polkinghorne recently said that every scientific theory must be "tough, surprising and exciting" or it probably isn't true.[3] The same holds true for the way we think about the anguish and mystery of unanswered prayer. Any "theory," any attempt to explain it, must be tough, surprising and exciting because the "answers" aren't quick or easy.

Why should we start exploring the mystery of unanswered prayer with Psalm 88? Won't this just undermine our faith? Apparently (since this is God's living Word to us), God isn't threatened by my honest questions. God knows that sometimes my life feels and looks like Psalm 88. If you're anything like me, you've probably had Psalm 88 moments, and if you haven't had them, you will have them.

For some reason this gives me comfort: God views the mystery of unanswered prayer with the utmost seriousness. God doesn't fear my questions and my dark emotions. God even provides the words I need to express my agony back to him.

EXCAVATING THE HEART

Of course, the reality of Psalm 88 doesn't take me off the hook entirely. Yes, prayer is mysterious, but that doesn't imply that I can throw up my hands and say, "Yep, you see, it's all God's fault." At times the mystery of unanswered prayer intersects with my dysfunctional, self-centered approach to God and prayer.

In the biblical story no one provides a better example of this than Jonah. As I read through Jonah in one sitting, I noticed that Jonah prays all the time. Unfortunately, most of his prayers are shallow, petty and self-serving. Some of his prayers seem deep and sincere, but they never actually change Jonah's heart. By the end of the story, he's still a mean and surly prophet of the Lord. Jonah wants God to incinerate the Ninevites, the brutal enemies of Jonah's people. Instead, God shows mercy and allows them to repent. This makes Jonah "greatly displeased" and "angry" (Jonah 4:1). He's so cranky that his prayer request boils down to a very unfunny one-liner: "Now, O LORD, take away my life, for it is better for me to die than to live" (Jonah 4:3). As far as prayers go, it's direct and bold; it's a cry for help from a desperate place. But it's also laced with anger, self-pity and immaturity. So rather than granting Jonah's request, God simply says, "Have you any right to be angry?" (Jonah 4:4).

Then God sends a plant to provide shade over Jonah's head in the hot desert sun. Jonah's prayers have been answered before he even mouths the prayer request. Ah, at last, God is acting reasonably, finally lining up with Jonah's agenda. Then God destroys the plant and lets Jonah sulk in the hot sun. Once again Jonah stomps his feet and lashes out at God. Jonah's heart bobs like a piece of driftwood floating in the ocean: when the tide is up, he's up; when the tide is down, he goes down. When God arranges the circumstances of his life to his liking, Jonah is happy; when the circumstances don't line up according to Jonah's wishes, he's a royal pain in the neck.

It's obvious to me that Jonah acts like a ridiculous human being and that his prayers are puny and pathetic. But then I have to ask myself: from God's perspective, do my prayers—even some of my prettiest and most "God-honoring" prayers—look like Jonah's prayers? Apparently they do, because God would say later in the New Testament book of James, "What causes fights and quarrels among you? Don't they come from *your* desires that battle within *you?*" (James 4:1, emphasis added). Personally, I don't appreciate those nasty pronouns "your" and "you." My gosh, this seems to resolve part of the mystery of unanswered prayer by pointing an accusing finger right in my face. But James isn't done yet. He also turns a spotlight on my prayers: "When you ask, you do not receive, because you ask with wrong motives, that you may spend what you get on your pleasures" (James 4:3). The punch line comes next: "You adulterous people, don't you know that friendship with the world is hatred toward God?" (James 4:4).

I don't like these accusations, but at times they're true. Author Jerry Sittser once said, "Unanswered prayers excavate our hearts." In other words, unanswered prayers function as a gigantic bulldozer, striking and plowing up the surface of our heart, uncovering a cesspool brimming with the raw sewage of my own selfishness. So, yes, there is a mystery to unanswered prayer. But my prayers (at their worst moments) reek with my own agenda; and my prayers (even in their best moments) have a very limited scope and agenda.

We probably don't have to think too long before we're hit with specific examples. We pray for a parking spot, which means that if God grants our request, ten other harried drivers won't get the spot. We pray for our children to ace the test, but it's graded on a curve, which means that someone else's child will fail. We pray for our nation to bomb another nation, knowing full well that there are six hundred thousand confessing Christians in that country who are praying for protection. We pray to be delivered from temptation and lust, but we never really want to let go of the pleasure it brings. We're like St. Augustine who in his *Confessions* prayed that God would deliver him from lust—but not yet. We quote Mark 11:24 ("whatever you ask for in prayer, believe that you have received it, and it will be yours"), but then we ignore the next verse: "And when you stand praying, if you hold anything against anyone, forgive him, so that your Father in heaven may forgive you" (Mark 11:25).

So as I'm trying to pray with boldness and confidence, I'm also remembering one of God's objectives in my prayers: God wants to change me, not just my circumstances. Sometimes God chooses to remove and revise my circumstances; sometimes God chooses to leave my circumstances so he can *revise me.* Jonah wanted God to change his circumstances, to annihilate the Ninevites, to give him a nice shade tree. But God wanted to change Jonah, to excavate his heart by removing his self-pity, his lack of love and his pettiness.

I recall a friend of mine telling me that for the first twenty years of her marriage she consistently prayed that God would change her husband. My friend had a long list of suggestions and ideas for how God could answer her heartfelt prayer. Some of them were "correct" prayers: her husband wasn't abusive, but he was certainly immature, driven and insensitive. And who knew the guy's faults better than his wife? But after twenty years of banging her head against God's unanswered prayer, she finally started asking God to change her. Amazingly enough, when she asked God to excavate her heart, God transformed her. Eventually God changed her husband too, but that's not the point of this story. The point is that God wanted to plow up and change her judgment-laced, unhappy, husband-focused heart.

In the same way, I've started to notice that as soon as I pray, *God, why won't you change my wife, my kids, my coworkers, my job, my finances, my neighbor, my leaders, my health, my depression, my temptations, so that I can be happier and serve you better?* God seems to respond by saying, "I want to change you through these circumstances." This will always appear cruel unless I remember God's overarching purpose for my life: to make us like Christ (see Romans 8:28-29). All of God's work for good on my behalf is directed toward that goal.

Once I accept that God is for me, that God is even consumed with a fierce and jealous love for me, working for his glory and my deepest happiness—then I begin to look at some of my unanswered prayers in a different light. God might be using unanswered prayers as the giant blade that's designed to excavate my heart.

That gives me a very different perspective on my prayer life. As I look at my unanswered prayers from God's perspective, I may no longer ask, how will God arrange the circumstances of my life to meet my needs and line up with my agenda? Now the question becomes much more complicated and mysterious: how will God take the prayers of millions of people and work a zillion fragments of circumstances to somehow make it all work out for his glory and for our good over a lifetime and for all eternity? I won't even attempt an answer to that question, but that's the real question behind unanswered prayer.

So when I pray for that "magic" parking spot, God may vaporize a car to make a space for me, or he may just allow me to drive in circles for another twenty minutes. Either way he's still working for my good. And maybe by forcing me to drive another twenty minutes, he'll dredge up and excavate some ugly selfishness from my heart.

SOMETHING BETTER THAN ANSWERED PRAYERS

But God doesn't revise us without giving us the strength and grace first. Sometimes God gives us something better than answered prayer: himself. That's exactly what Paul claimed in 2 Corinthians 12:7-10. Paul was writing to a group of Christians who were very impressed with marvelous displays of God's power: miracles, speaking in tongues, flashy displays of brilliance and intellectualism. Paul had performed some pretty impressive miracles in his day (see Romans 15:18-19). But at this point in the letter he mentions a small, quiet, humbling story: Paul, the great leader, the great miracle worker, the great warrior of prayer, had a problem. A "thorn" had lodged in his flesh. Whatever the thorn was, it didn't appear to be God's will. Paul called it "a messenger of Satan." So three times he pleaded with God to remove it, get rid of it, take it away. And three times God said no.

God gave Paul something else instead. God said, "My grace is sufficient for you, for my power is made perfect in weakness." God answered Paul's prayer; but rather than remove the thorn, God gave Paul his own power and presence.

Honestly, this all sounds grand in theory, but whenever I've had a huge thorn lodged in my soul, I just want it taken out. At times my prayers have not been, *Thank you, God, for more of your power* but *This is not a good deal, so I just want out of suffering. I want the thorn removed. And while you're at it, I want the promotion or the bigger home or a lover or the marriage saved or my child to get straight A's or a new car or world peace or a healthy baby or . . .* But in spite of my wishes, I've noticed that the Bible has a very different perspective. God made us and wired us to crave and even pant after him (see Psalm 42:1-2; 63:1-2). I'm always longing for God, even when I'm not aware of it. So every time I pray, I'm not merely praying to get something; I'm praying to be with Someone.

Jerry Sittser writes movingly about this truth in his book titled *When God Doesn't Answer Your Prayers.* In one day—in an instant, actually—his life changed forever. A drunk driver careened across the center line and struck the van driven by Jerry's wife, killing her, their four-year-old daughter and Jerry's mother. As Jerry struggled with the anguish of this tragedy, after a number of years he realized that his heart hungered for something even greater than the gifts of God: he wanted the presence of God. On a human level that's exactly what he missed from his wife. He missed her presence, not just her gifts and the duties she performed for him. Sittser wrote:

> After the accident I missed Lynda for many reasons. . . . At first I wished she were still alive to help keep my life going at home. I needed her, at least in part, to do chores . . . to drive the kids to their activities. But I have long since mastered those responsibilities. . . . Yet the ache remains because I miss *her,* not for what she could do but for who she is. I don't miss a wife in the abstract; I miss the person I was married to. I still see her face. . . . I still miss our late-night conversations. I even miss the fights. I have come to learn that the real pain of widowhood is the loss of the relationship with the one person I had given my heart to.[4]

In the same way that he longed for his wife, Jerry Sittser realized that he had an even deeper longing for God. Spiritually speaking, he didn't just want God to perform "chores" for him; he wanted to see God's face, and he desired to meet God for "late-night conversations."

The apostle Paul discovered the same truth. Prayer is not getting stuff from God; it's being with God, as a child is with her Father. Once again, this isn't the message I always want to hear, but I'm slowly concluding that God sometimes grants us the gift of unanswered prayers so we can find something even better than answers: God wants us to know the Giver, not just the gifts. Unfortunately, I often have to take a long, hard journey to discover that my thorns and my weaknesses are sometimes better teachers than my triumphs and trophies. It's strange, but sometimes when I've stretched out my hands and asked for a good gift from my Father, he's left me empty-handed. But in the midst of my emptiness and powerlessness, God always shows up in ways I never imagined.

WHEN God DIDN'T ANSWER God

Perhaps the most shocking unanswered prayer that I found in the Bible comes from the lips of Jesus himself. Right before he went to the cross, Jesus entered the garden of Gethsemane and prayed: "'*Abba*, Father,' he said, 'everything is possible for you. Take this cup from me'" (Mark 14:36, emphasis in original). We know from the other Gospels that Jesus prayed this with persistence and with passion. He asked with intensity, so much so that he sweated great drops of blood (Luke 22:44). Jesus also prayed with trust and confidence. He fully believed that his heavenly Father could have sent thousands of angels to rescue him (see Matthew 26:53). And yet we also know that this specific request ("Take this cup from me") went unanswered. Jesus hung on the cross anyway.

I've often struggled with what to make of this unanswered prayer. First of all, I noticed that Jesus added a small but powerful addendum on to his prayer: "Yet not what I will, but what you will" (Mark 14:36). Ultimately, Jesus wanted one thing more than getting his way: he wanted the perfect, difficult, sweet will of his Father. Jesus, as the One who lived the life we should have lived, shows us how to "do" prayer: pray honestly, specifically, boldly, passionately; but pray for one thing—God's will. As someone has said, for Jesus prayer is like a blank check that requires two signatures instead of one. We sign it, we ask, we pray big and bold, but then we know that God the Father must countersign the check.

Of course, there's something else that astounds me in this story: Jesus is not only perfectly human, he's also perfectly God. So in this scenario in the garden, it's accurate to say that God the Father did not answer the prayer of God the Son. Jesus, who is God in human flesh, knows about unanswered prayer. In other words, just like us, God has experienced unanswered prayer.

A few years ago my friend Bill brought this truth home to me in an unforgettable way. Actually Bill clings to this unanswered prayer of Jesus with a ferocious tenderness. About forty years ago Bill and his wife, Sandra, lost a son when he tragically drowned. When I preached on Jesus' unanswered prayer in the garden, I thought I talked with passion and power . . . until I met Bill. During the next week Bill and I met for lunch, and he explained to me the real nature of this story.

With fervency and gentleness Bill looked me in the eye and said, "This is the most tender passage in the whole Bible. God the Son cries out to God the Father, and his prayer isn't answered. Jesus will go to the cross. He will drink the cup. He will suffer and die, but the greatest suffering is this: God the Son, the One who has for all eternity been united with his Father, will experience the utter horror of separation from his Father. It will taste like hell. So it's as if God the Son cries out, 'Papa, help me, but I'll do this for you and for them. I'll miss you, Papa, but if this is the only way to save the world, I will drink the cup to the dregs.' So you see, Matt, he did this for us. His prayer went unanswered, but it was the only way to obey the Father and to save his lost creation."

Bill taught me a profound lesson. Unanswered prayer is a mystery and a "problem." It causes anguish. The answers don't always come quickly, and sometimes they don't seem to come at all. If I believed that God was basically against me, a counterweight to my happiness, the dreaded, much-feared, terrible, unpredictable Lord and Master of the universe, unanswered prayers would frustrate and sadden me. But if I really begin to see God's good heart, that through Christ and in Christ, God is for me and not against me, then I can trust God's good heart. When I look at the cross, the place where God was willing to go for us, I can declare, "I may not understand many things. I do not understand prayer—why and how and when God answers prayer. But as I look at the cross, I have no doubt that God is for me."

Oh, by the way, do you remember my friend Susan, who prayed and had the bird poop dropped on her head? Looking back on the experience of her unanswered prayer, Susan realizes that in a quirky and comical way, the bird poop was an answer to prayer. Seven years ago during her struggle with depression, she continued a slow descent into the darkness. But surprisingly that day on the beach marked a profound change in her life. She started to emerge from the darkness that gripped her heart.

When I asked Susan how God answered her prayer with a glob of bird poop, she said, "It was as if God told me, 'Look, you asked for a sign, so the sign is this: you've just hit bottom. It can't get any more "bottom" than this. I, the Lord your God, won't allow you to sink any lower than this. As a matter of fact, today is the last day of sinking down into depression.' It was a slow ascent, but it was also the beginning of a renewed healing in my life."

How does God use bird poop to answer a prayer? I don't know. The questions get even bigger and more mysterious, questions like *How does God use a cross to lead us into resurrection?* I really don't know.

Sometimes prayers do seem to go unanswered. I've mentioned just four examples of unanswered prayer, but there are certainly more possibilities. As I said, I do not have a grand, unified theory of unanswered prayer. It's a mystery to me, and so is God. But I do know that God is good. I do know that God is sovereign in his purposes and diligent in his plan to save and bless us. He is for me, and he is certainly for you. Sometimes that's the only theory we have.

5

PRAYER AS ABSENCE

For many years my prayer life operated with a simple formula: Prayer + Faith = The Presence of God. In other words, when I pray, I'm supposed to *feel* closer to God. According to my spiritual tradition, I should feel my heart "strangely warmed" by God's presence.[1] At the very least, prayer shouldn't make me feel more of God's absence.

That's the way it's supposed to work. Unfortunately, the formula hasn't always fit real life—for me or for others I love. It didn't work for a good friend of mine. At this point in his life, he feels more of God's absence than God's presence. After pouring his sweat and time and money into a new church, the church disintegrated amidst charges of gossip and power plays. People in the church started accusing and then hating each other. My friend's teenage daughter watched all these "mature Christians" fight and hurt each other until she finally said, "I've had it. I'm leaving church and God for good." So she walked out of their lives and started down a destructive path of addictions. My friend fell into a deep depression. He lost his daughter, his church, most of his friends and his connection with God. Where's the sweetness of God's presence? Why did God allow everything to blow up?

I was also shocked to discover that the formula wasn't even a good fit for Mother Teresa. Apparently she never experienced the overt disappointment and hurt that my friend did; instead, Mother Teresa just felt far from God. In December of 1979, as she accepted the Nobel Peace Prize, she delivered the upbeat and stirring message that the world had come to expect from the "Saint of the Gutters." She told her audience that the Christmas holiday should remind us "that the radiating joy is real" because Christ is everywhere—"Christ in our hearts, Christ in the poor we meet, Christ in the smile we give and in the smile we receive." In sharp contrast, less than three months earlier Mother Teresa had written to a friend about the darkness of her faith: "Jesus has a very special love for you, . . . [but] as for me, the silence and the emptiness is so great, I look and do not see . . . the tongue moves [in prayer] but does not speak." In a series of letters written over sixty-six years, she often mentioned her state of spiritual dryness, darkness and loneliness.[2]

What happened to my friend's faith? What happened in Mother Teresa's prayer life? What happens when we pray—honestly, faithfully, passionately—and God still feels far away? When we encounter these seasons of dryness and God-absence, has the mechanism of prayer broken down? If so, whose fault is it?

In my experience, we don't like to talk about these strangely cold seasons of our spiritual journey with Christ. God is *supposed* to feel close to us. So the felt absence of God propels us into a personal crisis and a potential public-relations fiasco. God feels far away, but don't let the secret out. What would our friends think? It certainly won't help promote the image of the victorious and happy Jesus-follower who vanquishes adversity and keeps smiling through the dark seasons of life.

As I've struggled through my own times of God's felt absence, I've discovered that the Bible doesn't engage in a P.R. spin for God. According to the biblical record, some of God's closest friends experienced dire seasons when God seemed far away. For example, Psalm 42 was written by a man who was passionately pursuing God. He wasn't a casual "seeker"; he was like a deer desperately panting for water: "As the deer pants for streams of water, so my soul pants for you, O God. My soul thirsts for God, for the living God. When can I go and meet with God?" (Psalm 42:1-2).

He's in a spiritual desert, a dry and thirsty place. At one time he felt very close to God: "I used to go with the multitude, leading the procession to the house of God, with shouts of joy and thanksgiving among the festive throng" (Psalm 42:4). Those were the good old days! But now, overcome by the weight of God-absence, he simply cries out, "My tears have been my food day and night" (Psalm 42:3).

That strikes me as a strange prayer from someone who was passionately seeking God. According to my original prayer formula (Prayer + Faith = The Presence of God), he should say, "Because I've panted for you, O God, you have filled me with gladness and my heart feels 'strangely warmed.'" Instead he prays, "Why have you forgotten me? Why must I go about mourning . . . ? My bones suffer mortal agony as my foes taunt me, saying to me all day long, 'Where is your God?'" (Psalm 42:9-10). Rather than feeling embraced by the warmth of God's presence, this ancient and sincere seeker after God felt only the cold, dark space of God's absence.

UNDERSTANDING THE "ABSENCE" OF GOD

How do we understand these seasons of desolation? When God feels far away, I've tended to limit myself to one of three options: (1) God isn't doing his job. (2) I'm not doing my job. (3) Life isn't doing its job. Options two and three are definitely possibilities, but when they don't fit my experience, I'm glad that the tradition of Christian prayer provides another ancient option.

A few years ago, quite by accident, I discovered one of these older, wiser guides for the painful and lonely journey through God-thirsty times. We know him today as St. John of the Cross. I tried to read him about ten years ago, but I just got bored with his seemingly dreary analysis of the spiritual journey. But after I went through a profound and painful season of feeling God's absence and darkness, St. John started to resonate with my soul. John seemed to be one of the few Christians who dared to tell me, "Your original formula doesn't work. There will be times when God feels far away. That is a normal condition of your spiritual journey. But don't give up, because these 'dark nights of the soul' are actually a beautiful gift from your heavenly Father. Yes, my friend, experience the 'sheer grace of God's felt absence."

I started to admire John's writing because it wasn't just an academic tome. He clearly understood the spiritual drought the psalmist prayed about in Psalm 42. Shortly after his birth in Spain in 1542, John's father died suddenly. His mother labored to keep the family together, but John learned early that life can take tragic turns that force us to ask, "God, where are you in the midst of this pain?" At the age of twenty-six John became a spiritual leader in the church. As he was using his skills to reform the church, some of the church's leaders in Spain bristled with anger and suspicion. After warnings and threats, on a cold night in December an opposing group of Christians raided John's home in Avila, escorting him to a prison cell for interrogation and then imprisonment. Confined to a tiny, dirty, solitary closet, John endured malnutrition, putrid clothing and lice. In terms of his relationship with God, he said it was like the whale swallowing Jonah, "being digested in its lugubrious belly."[3]

These were some of the worst days of John's life. Everything went dark for John, and God felt far away. After all, it's one thing to be persecuted for your faith, to endure pain and disappointment, but John was abandoned and abused by other Christians. That doubled his pain and isolation. In one of his works of poetry, John would cry out to God, "Where have you hidden, Beloved, and left me moaning? You fled like a stag after wounding me; I went out calling, but you were gone."[4] Later, John would coin a phrase for this experience of feeling God's absence: "the dark night of the soul."

A friend of mine has likened the wounding of the dark night to hitting a wall at sixty miles per hour. For a while our life cruises along predictably, we feel in control of our circumstances, and the "God-road" we're driving on seems smooth and accessible. But then our life hits a wall we didn't expect and we can't get around. For St. John of the Cross, the wall (or the "whale's belly") was his unjust imprisonment and physical pain. For us the wall might be a divorce, a prolonged illness, a painful relationship, a deep depression or, like Mother

Teresa, just a long season of spiritual dryness. We pray; we cry out; we ask others to pray for us, but nothing happens. The satisfaction and comfort we once guzzled from God's fountain of grace suddenly dries up. Like the psalmist in Psalm 42, we're *supposed* to be happy; we're *supposed* to shout for joy with the "festive throng." We don't want to admit it to anyone else, but the "good days" are a distant dream; night has fallen, and God has turned the lights out.

Through his dusty writings, John mentored me in my prayer life. Initially John's writings didn't fit my assumptions about prayer. Nor would he fit with many contemporary expressions of the spiritual life. For the most part, we'd rather keep our worship services beating with happy tunes and shining with bright lights. But John taught me that any authentic spirituality must grapple with the dark side of life. We *do* feel far from God sometimes. Surprisingly, John argued that in these times of God's felt absence, God may be much closer than we ever imagined. It's often when our life seems to be unraveling that God is putting us back together again. It's often in the deserts of life that God pours his deep satisfaction into our souls. But how does that make sense? How does unraveling suggest reconstructing? How does dryness lead to infilling?

THE PILLOW OR THE FLAME?

First of all, John would bring our prayer life back to the character of God. He wouldn't put it in these terms, but I will: take the following multiple-choice quiz. Choose one correct answer for each question:

1. God is more like
   A. a soft down pillow for our weary head
   B. a flamethrower spitting out fire aimed at our chest

2. God is more likely to say
   A. "I'm here whenever you need to snuggle up, get cozy and take a nap."
   B. "Come over here and let me singe you and burn up all the garbage in your heart."

If you chose answer A for either of these questions, based on my understanding of John's writings, he might say something like, "Sorry, wrong answer, my friend. Yes, God is love. Yes, God acts like the pillow—warm, soft, inviting. Yes, Jesus promises us true rest. But according to the Bible, God is more like the flamethrower aimed at our chest, prepared to singe the garbage in our lives." All throughout his writings John utilizes one overarching image for God's love: a living, vibrant flame. But God's love isn't out of control. God doesn't consume us in anger; he refines us in his perfect love. "Flame, fire, blazing, burning. . . . The Spirit John knows is an 'infinite fire of love,' able to set the heart 'blazing more intensely than all the fire in the world.'"[5]

This helped me understand some of those severe passages in the Bible, like Hebrews 12:29, which picture God as "a consuming fire." Of course, God isn't a reckless flamethrower. God always has a goal in mind with his flame of love: he wants to refine us. The Bible tells us that we matter so much to God that we are God's masterpiece, God's work of art (see Ephesians 2:10). God the flamethrower never intends to hurt us and destroy us; he always intends to make us glorious—or in John's native Spanish, God wants to make us *grande*. As a matter of fact, God wants to keep burning away the dross in our lives until we look and act like a glorious, fully redeemed, utterly *grande* image of Jesus Christ (see Romans 8:29).

This process of refinement by fire certainly wasn't foreign to my life. As a father of four children, I feel the same way about my kids. I labor to refine them, to make them mature and whole, decent and kind. So even as an imperfect parent, on some days I'm like a soft pillow but on other days I need to act like a consuming fire.

Friends sometimes need to act like a flame as well. If you have a good friend who is addicted to alcohol, you can't always act like the soft, fluffy pillow type of friend; sometimes you may have to confront your friend, "speaking the truth in love" (Ephesians 4:15). The truth may burn deep, but your goal is always to refine your friend's life. In the same way God, the living flame of love, wants to transform and refine us.

WE NEEd THE GARBAGE MAN

Second, John taught me that before I could understand my "dark nights," I needed to know something about myself: there's garbage strewn in my heart. Someone has to rummage through my heart, find the garbage, take out the trash and burn it. In his infinite love and concern for us, God volunteers to serve as our garbage man and personal soul-incinerator. That's a harsh way to say it, and John used a nicer word than garbage—he referred to our "imperfections." It doesn't really matter—garbage or imperfections, it's hard for me to admit that I have either. I'd rather nominate myself for the gifted, fast-track group of Jesus-students. But because we all have such massive piles of spiritual imperfections, we'll remain spiritual beginners for a long, long time. Perhaps that's what Jesus meant when he proclaimed, "Blessed are the poor in spirit, for theirs is the kingdom of heaven" (Matthew 5:3).

It's one thing to admit that, yes, theoretically and theologically I'm a beginner and even a sinner; but it's quite another to own up to the specific traits that expose and lay bare my sin and immaturity. By exploring the classic "deadly sins," John exposed the concrete ways I display a beginner status in my prayer life. This is the garbage that needs to get hauled out of my heart.

What do beginners act like? John lists some of their telltale faults:

Pride. We become sad when we see our own faults because we want the quick path to sainthood; we're too embarrassed to face and confess our sins; as beginners we're very picky about who can teach or lead us (e.g., "I can't learn unless so-and-so is teaching, and I can't worship unless so-and-so is leading or unless the music meets my standards").

Spiritual greed. According to John, "[Beginners] will hardly ever seem content with the spirit God gives them. They become unhappy and peevish because they don't find the consolation they want in spiritual things." We'll spend more time attending Bible studies and reading books about God than actually acting more like Jesus. As beginners we're forever filtering our spiritual food—sermons, worship

?

services, Bible studies, even our personal prayer times—through the grid of one question: Did I get fed?

Anger. "[Beginners] become angry over the sins of others, reprove these others, and sometimes even feel the impulse to do so angrily . . . setting themselves up as lord of virtue." Sometimes we "are so unbearable that no one can put up with [us]." Or we'll become impatient and angry with our own imperfections, demanding to be saints in a day.

Spiritual gluttony. Beginners "strive more for spiritual savor than for spiritual purity." In our terms today, we'd choose our guitar-driven worship songs or organ-led hymns ahead of actual spiritual transformation in Christ.

Spiritual envy. As beginners we feel sad when we hear about others who zip past us on the spiritual journey. We can't rejoice with those who rejoice.

Spiritual sloth. Spiritual challenges easily overwhelm or bore the beginner. "Since they are so used to finding delight in spiritual exercises, they become bored when they do not find it. If they do not receive in prayer the satisfaction they crave . . . they do not want to return to it, or at times they either give up prayer or go to it begrudgingly."[6]

It's not an exhaustive list of imperfections, but this list certainly pierces through my armor of "spiritual maturity." As I read John's writings, I reluctantly concluded that I'm still a bona fide beginner in the spiritual life and I'll remain a beginner for a long time. But of course the gospel is all about good news: God, my gentle garbage man, wants to drag out my imperfections so he can forgive them and then slowly burn them away. That's why John called God "the living flame of love that tenderly wounds my soul in its deepest center."[7] I was discovering that God seeks a radical cure for my disease. God doesn't settle for tidying up the outer surface of my life; he'll clean me up from the inside out.

Adjusting to Night Vision

How does God clean us up from the inside out? From John of the

Cross I learned that God often uses the dark nights of my soul to burn away my imperfections. A flame suggests something about God; a dark night suggests something about our spiritual journey.

So what does a dark night look like? Although nights aren't necessarily filled with dread, they do impart a sense of disorientation and a loss of control. Whenever I wake up in the middle of the night, usually fretting over some issue or a huge list of concerns, I seldom get clarity. Usually the nighttime, with its deep and eerie silence, just makes me more anxious. My mind starts racing and my heart beats faster. I can't think straight, and I usually decide, "I just have to wait for the morning, and then maybe I can straighten everything out." In the same way, the dark nights of our spiritual lives make us feel disoriented, even like we're unraveling. John defined a dark night as those times when it feels like "everything and everyone is failing you . . . it also seems like God is failing you . . . [and] everything seems to be functioning in reverse."[8]

Dark nights also suggest a loss of control. In other words, we can't fix and control our dark nights. The ancient prayer in Psalm 42 reflects a loss of control. The psalmist was stuck in exile, and he desperately wanted to trek home so he could enjoy the good old days. But he couldn't fix or control the process. Again, when I wake up in the middle of the night disoriented and anxious, I want to force the morning to come faster. "Just get me out of this eerie, lonely nighttime," I demand. It doesn't work because I'm not in charge of the night. Spiritually speaking, I usually don't ask God for dark nights; God just sends them.

This is often painful for us because we like to control everything we can. We like to have the answers for all of our questions. We want everything to make sense right now. We want our unraveled lives to come together right now. As we sometimes say, we like to take the bull by the horns. That's a great image for our desire to control everything, including the "wild bull" of our spiritual journey. But in our dark nights of the soul, God begins to lead us in a way that's beyond our control.

John uses the image of a man who embarks on a journey to unknown lands. He's forced to follow a new route, and he doesn't have the right maps. Our traveler must leave his old familiar paths and travel by a strange and unfamiliar route. The old maps that he thought he could trust don't seem to work anymore. This journey feels scary and confusing. In the same way, the dark nights of our spiritual times, those seasons when God invites us to follow him without the right maps into the darkness along a strange route, can feel frightening and perhaps even senseless. At times we say, "If I knew God was in it, I could make this journey with ease." But that's the point of dark nights of the soul: it doesn't *feel* like God is in it. That is what makes it the night.

For most of my spiritual journey with Christ, I've possessed reliable maps as I've traveled on an adventurous but predictable route. But a few years ago I entered a dark night in which all my old maps became inadequate. At this point in my life, it's too painful to share the details; I just knew that God felt far away. As a matter of fact, every time I prayed for something specific, God "answered" my prayers by doing the exact opposite of what I wanted. It was uncanny how God stripped me of my maps. While my life slowly unraveled in the dark night, God seemed to ditch me. I felt like the psalmist: "I used to go with the multitude, leading the procession to the house of God, with shouts of joy and thanksgiving among the festive throng."

In the midst of this crisis, John's strange and dreary writings finally started to make sense. John of the Cross reframed this experience for me by pointing to a deeper, Bible-based framework for these questions. "God has not abandoned you," John would say. "You aren't experiencing God's real absence; you are merely experiencing God's presence in a whole new way. Just like the presence of the sun overwhelms our senses, so the presence of God is so bright that it blinds your spiritual sight and makes you feel like you're in the dark. In the midst of this dark night, in the midst of this powerlessness and confusion, in the midst of the felt absence of God, as you feel like you're heading in reverse, God, the Living Flame, the Fire of Holy Love, is refining your imperfections. God is closer than you could imagine."

WHEN God TAKES MY MILK AWAY

John used a number of beautiful images to describe God's good work during our dark nights. My favorite was his picture of a mother (God) and her nursing child (us). When the child is being weaned, he may feel like the mother has abandoned him. But of course we know that the mother is merely helping the child to grow up and walk for himself. John tells us that our relationship with God works the same way. In the initial stages of our life in Christ, God often offers us "sweet and satisfying spiritual milk." We don't even have to work for it; it just flows into us. But when God senses that we need to grow up, God withdraws the accessible liquid comfort, puts us on the ground and teaches us to walk and leave our babyish outlook behind. Naturally the baby "finds this new phase bewildering, since everything has turned back-to-front."[9] The baby cries, stamps his feet and demands to have his milk back.

It's the same way in our spiritual life. In our dark nights it feels like God has just taken something away from us. So we cry and stamp our feet and demand that God give us our milk back. But, again, God isn't absent; he just *feels* absent to us. God is actually working deep in our heart to burn up our imperfections and cause us to trust in him even without his milk. So John would warn, "Do not be like the many foolish ones who, in their lowly understanding of God, think that when they do not understand, taste, or experience him, he is far away and utterly concealed. The contrary belief would be truer."[10]

Our problem is that we associate the milk with God. "Milk" could be anything that the synapses in our brain connect with "God." It could be a certain style of music, the people we're fond of, special places or cities, a particular climate, a church building or a specific church architecture, a certain preacher or author, or a special prayer method. We demand to have these things. So, for example, when we lose our style of music, we not only grieve (which may be appropriate), but we also stamp our feet and demand that we get it back.

I take in my "milk" every morning as I pray and read my Bible with a cup of hot Starbucks coffee (it has to be really hot or I can't pray) and sit under an apple tree in our city's bird sanctuary. It's part of my routine to connect with God, and the synapses in my brain crave this routine. One fine morning a rude and spiritually obtuse city employee came to the park with his chainsaw, wreaking havoc and interrupting my prayer time. I wanted to scream over the chain saw, "Hey, you can't do that now. Can't you see my Bible and my hot coffee? This is my time with God. Gosh, how dense can you get?"

But as I reflect on this, I now realize how much "my time with God" is just my milk. At times God will take my milk away—for short seasons or permanently—in order to remind me that God isn't the milk. God will remove the milk so I can know *him*, not just my good feelings or nice experiences about God. God will withdraw the liquid comfort, the fast and easy spiritual meals I crave, replacing it with solid food. God is the solid food. He's the One I hunger for.

LIVING WITH AN "ABSENT" GOD

So how have these images—God the Flame and the dark nights of the soul—changed my life? I still don't *like* dark nights, nor do I ask for them; on the other hand, I have the more realistic view that they will come to me. At some point most of us will experience times of dryness and desolation. It many not be tied to a crisis; but then again, it may involve a specific life event: a marriage disintegrates even when we pray for healing; a loved one dies, leaving a gaping wound in our heart; a child slides into spiritual darkness and addiction; a job turns sour for reasons beyond our control; cancer returns; our church family ceases to fill us with delight; old age continues to drag us downward; the baby or the marriage partner we long for doesn't come. An ache settles into the bottom of our gut, and it won't go away. In bewilderment we quietly ask, "Where is God?"

I am learning a few profound lessons about these dark nights of my journey with Christ.

I'm learning to admit when I'm in a dark night. A dark night isn't just a trial. Most of us aren't ashamed of trials. When Paul went through trials, he confidently proclaimed, "We also rejoice in our sufferings" (Romans 5:3); but when he encountered a dark night, he confessed, "We were under great pressure, far beyond our ability to endure, so that we despaired even of life" (2 Corinthians 1:8). It's hard for us to hear our spiritual leaders honestly share their dark-night encounters, but Paul certainly did it. So when I feel more of God's absence than God's presence, I'm learning to say, "I'm in a dark night. It feels bewildering and disorienting; I've slammed into a wall. I don't know what God is doing in my life and sometimes my only prayer is, *God, where are you?*" That isn't whining; that's honest, psalm-saturated, Jesus-modeled praying.

I'm learning that God hasn't abandoned me in my dark-night experiences. I can lean on Jesus' promise to never fail or forsake me (Matthew 28:20). But Jesus didn't just speak a promise. As he died on the cross for our sakes, he lived the promise and demonstrated his faith in the promise. Our dark nights often feel senseless and lonely. We cry out "Why, God?" and "How long, O Lord?" and "Where are you in the midst of this suffering?" But I'm receiving comfort in the fact that Jesus himself, my brother (Hebrews 2:11), also cried out from inside a dark night: "My God, my God, why have you forsaken me?" (Matthew 27:46). Jesus walked through not just a dark night but what John of the Cross called the *horrenda noche,* or "the terrible night." The Bible doesn't provide an exhaustive answer to all of my big "Why?" questions, but it does tell me that God has plunged into every form of dark night. Thus, no matter how deep my nights take me, God has descended deeper into the dark night of human suffering.

I'm discovering that God has a good plan for me in the midst of my dark nights. His hand is sovereign, and it is good (see Romans 8:28; Philippians 1:6; Genesis 50:20). In another masterful illustration, John likened a dark night to the cure given to a sick man. When someone is sick, the house must be hushed. The food is simple and dull: dry toast, bland broth, ice chips. Friends and family members must withdraw from the sick man. In the midst of his delirium and struggle for health, the sick man may feel abandoned and alone. But it's the "darkness" of his circumstances that allow the sick man to become whole. In the same way, John would argue, when we walk through a spiritual dark-night experience, our soul is "undergoing a cure, in order that it may regain its health—its health being God himself." God the Living Flame is burning away our imperfections; he is weaning us from our attachment to milk (our thoughts, feelings and experiences *about* God rather than God), so that God can truly be God in our lives.

I'm learning not to rush my dark nights. I can't control the nighttime; God does. John wrote with beauty and clarity about the central biblical goal of our spiritual lives: union with Jesus Christ, our Bridegroom. But the path we take and the God who leads us on that path are often mysterious. So John advised us, "Never stop with loving and delighting in your understanding and experience of God, but love and delight in what you cannot understand or experience of him. Such is the way . . . of seeking him in faith. . . . Thus in drawing near him, you will experience darkness because of the weakness of your eye."[11] In other words, the closer we get to God (or the closer God moves toward us) the more we're overwhelmed by the sheer wonder, glory and mystery of God's unfathomable presence—just as the closer we get to the sun, the more we're blinded by the sun's brilliance and heat. John tells us to enjoy the mystery and to worship the Mysterious One who is known in Jesus but is still so far beyond our ability to understand completely.

So when I'm tempted to tell God, "I can't have this dark night (e.g., of sickness or disappointment or spiritual dryness or rejection or grief); I'm too busy; I have important projects to do for you, Lord," God seems to say, "Your 'important projects' can wait a little while. I want to focus on my project for you: making you whole and mature in my Son, Jesus."

In these seasons I'm learning to ask for the "sheer grace" of the dark night: the gift of a loving heart. The Bible is clear about the final goal and destination of the spiritual journey in Christ: love. "If I speak in the tongues of men and of angels, but have not love, I am only a resounding gong or a clanging cymbal" (1 Corinthians 13:1). "The entire law is summed up in a single command: 'Love your neighbor as yourself'" (Galatians 5:14). According to John of the Cross, most of us are mere beginners on this journey toward love. Our hearts often petrify with a judgmental spirit. We become "lords of virtue" who often act like the older brother in Jesus' parable—angry, aloof and harsh (see Luke 15:25-32). But every time we encounter a dark night, God chips away at the hardness of unlove in our heart. Every time we hit a wall at sixty miles per hour, God breaks us down and then remakes us with a little more love in our hearts.

Once again, John the poet utilized a beautiful metaphor for our spiritual lives: we are like a smudged window. The sun may shine on the window, but the dirt merely blocks the sun from beaming through it. The dirt parallels all the barriers to love in our heart. But in the words of John, "A soul makes room for God by wiping away all the smudges and smears of creatures . . . for to love is to labor to divest and deprive oneself for God of all that is not God. When this is done the soul will be illumined by and transformed in God."[12] So in the dark night, when God seems to withdraw from us, God is working behind the scenes like a quiet window-washer man, silently but efficiently removing the smears until the beams of God's love shine into and then through us.

6

PRAYER AS AN ARGUMENT WITH GOD

Shortly after we moved from Minnesota, I met David, a Jewish follower of Jesus who constantly challenges me to view the Bible through Jewish eyes. David is also a passionate, brilliant, full-blooded New Yorker. For the first two years of my ministry on Long Island, David would often approach me after a worship service and begin with something like, "Hey, nice sermon, I liked that third point a lot, but I think you also missed something crucial in that passage. Let me tell you how I see this through Jewish eyes." And then he'd launch into his weekly five-minute rebuttal argument about the finer points of biblical exegesis. I thought he was trying to pick a fight with me, but I politely listened and thanked him for his "insights." After listening to his rebuttals for two years (Minnesotans are notoriously nice and long-suffering), I couldn't stand it anymore. So I finally blurted out, "David, what is the deal? Don't you get anything out of my sermons? Doesn't God tell you something? Why do you always come to me and critique my sermons? Why must you always nitpick about some minor point of theology?" My face flushed with anger and David stood there frozen in shock.

Finally David broke the icy silence. First, he laughed. Then he said,

"Maybe I should explain my cultural background, which is probably different than your ethnic background. When New York Jews like me argue about Scripture, we're asking for a dialogue. When I tell you that I disagree with something you've said, I'm expecting you to fire back and say, 'Oh yeah, well I think that you're wrong, too, and let me tell you why.' You see, Jewish people sometimes get close by arguing. Confronting each other is a sign of intimacy in the relationship. So when I dish it out, I want you to dish it right back. That's how the relationship grows."

This concept of achieving intimacy through intense dialogue and even a rousing argument was certainly new to me. But through my friendship with David, God has started to teach me an important lesson about prayer: sometimes prayer involves arguing with God. Sometimes we grow closer to God by "confronting" God.

My Jewish friends have known this for a long time. In her book on Jewish Midrash, Judith Kunst explains how Jewish people argue about Scripture: "A teacher announces the appointed Torah portion, but does not interpret it or even read it. Instead, all over the room, one *hevruta* (i.e., a friend or Torah study partner) begins to read the assigned section out loud. The other half listens intently (one would have to with so many voices raised in the room), then the other jumps in with a response, thus commencing an intense, often hours-long session of questioning, answering, arguing." So Kunst concludes, "In Judaism, intimacy cannot be separated from argument."[1]

Jews applied this idea (i.e., "intimacy cannot be separated from argument") to their prayer life as well. The Talmud states, "Boldness is effective—even against Heaven." There's a Yiddish story about a grandmother who took her grandson to an ocean beach. As the boy innocently played with his bucket and shovel in the sand by the ocean, a huge wave suddenly descended on the beach, swallowed the boy in its fury, and carried him out to sea. Every trace of the boy disappeared—his bucket, shovel and even his tiny hat. Panic-stricken and enraged, the grandmother started to pray: "Lord God of the universe, how can you allow such a thing to happen? My only grandson has been swallowed by a wave. You must not let him drown. With all due respect, I expect better treatment from you, Lord God. This is outrageous. Bring him back to me at once!" Suddenly another massive wave rolled in, dropped the boy unharmed on the beach and then receded into the ocean. For a moment the grandmother stared at the startled boy, and then she looked up at God and said, "Lord God, you know he also had a hat."

Like that grandmother, we pray confrontationally when we bring our questions and disagreements directly to God. Steeped in the Old Testament, Jewish people never cringed at the practice of arguing with God. A contemporary Jewish scholar states, "The Jewish literary heritage is replete with laments, dirges, complaints and arguments, all protesting God's treatment of His people."[2]

Intimacy cannot be separated from argument. This lesson has probably stretched me more than anything else in this book. For most of my life I've tried to avoid conflicts and arguments, which I've assumed are bad and scary and a sign of distance in a relationship. But this unique perspective on prayer is opening my life to greater health and honesty with God and others. People like my friend David are helping me practice this frightening but exciting way to pray.

"I WILL BE YOUR GOD"—SO WHERE DID YOU GO?

As I've started looking at the Bible through "Jewish lenses," I've discovered some of the unique angles on the character of God. God in the biblical story, unlike the gods of many world religions, is not distant, indifferent or even hostile and opposed to human happiness. Instead, the Bible reveals that God is good, and he rules the world with justice. God also made a covenant with his people by promising, "I will take you as my own people, and I will be your God" (Exodus 6:7). God bound himself to a specific people and then promised to care for them as they promised to obey and honor him. Both parties were connected by a binding, enduring love relationship.

The covenant plays a crucial role in prayers of confrontation. When God's people break the covenant, God accuses them of spiritual adultery. But there are times when God doesn't *seem* to be holding up his end of the covenant either. It *seems* like God is reneging on his side of the relationship. Obviously this is only a human perception, but God takes these perceptions seriously. From either side of this broken relationship, this leads to a confrontation.

The underlying framework of the covenant provides the pattern for prayers of confrontation, or what's also known as the "law court" pattern of prayer. The biblical law court pattern of prayer contains four movements:

1. An address to God.
2. The evidence. When things don't seem to line up with God's standard of justice, evidence is brought to and against God. God is the judge and the defendant, so the complaint is made *to* God and *against* God.
3. A specific request is made from God.
4. The response. God listens and responds. God agrees with the case or disagrees with the case, but either way, God responds to this law court process.

So as people like my friend David have mentored me in my prayer life, I'm learning that the covenant leads to confrontation. Most of the time God confronts us about our behavior. But because it's a real relationship and God desires intimacy with us, God also allows us to confront him about his behavior. We are allowed to make a case against God in order to come closer to God.

Sometimes our case bleeds like an open wound. The Hasidic Jews tell a story about a simple tailor who had a fight with God. His rabbi asked the tailor to recount the argument with God. The tailor said, "I declared to God: You wish me to repent of my sins. . . . But you, O Lord, have committed grievous sins: You have taken away babies from their mothers, and mothers from their babies. Let us be quits: You forgive me, and I will forgive you." The rabbi replied, "Why did you let God off so easily? You might have forced him to redeem all of Israel."[3]

Prayer as confrontation is an intense way to pray. Surprisingly, the Bible is filled with confrontational prayers. God not only allows it (he could suppress the prayers or just annihilate those who pray them), he seems to encourage it. When it's done with the right attitude and perspective, this pattern of prayer becomes God's passionate path for us to engage him. It's as if God is saying, "Talk, engage, respond to me. Anything is better than the silent treatment or the cold shoulder. Argue, rant, rave, yell, disagree, but don't just sit there. Or worse, don't come to me with pious, pretty words that are empty and fake." I'm learning that prayer is an intensely personal and passionate conversation with a covenant-making God who is there; it's an exercise that involves all of me—the real me, not just the pretty but pretend me.

HAULING GOD TO COURT

Since my blowup with David, I've started to discover that the Bible contains many examples of the principle called "intimacy through arguing." Apparently God also likes it when we dish it back to him every once in a while. The Bible is filled with believers who argue with God in raw, honest, earthy prayers of confrontation.

Abraham. The first example found in the Bible is when Abraham confronted God over God's planned destruction of Sodom and Gomorrah in Genesis 18. When God pulled Abraham aside and gave him an insider tip that he was going to destroy Sodom and Gomorrah, Abraham was saddened. But rather than wilt and sulk away from God, the biblical text tells us that Abraham "remained standing before the LORD" (Genesis 18:22). He didn't walk away; instead, he engaged God. And then Abraham started negotiating with God: "Will you sweep away the righteous with the wicked? What if there are fifty righteous people in the city? Will you really sweep it away and not spare the place for the sake of the fifty righteous people in it? Far be it from you to do such a thing. . . . Far be it from you! Will not the Judge of all the earth do right?" (Genesis 18:23-25).

As I reread this story, I noticed elements of the law court pattern of prayer at work in Abraham's bargaining session with God. Abraham was confronting God as judge and defendant based on God's standard of justice. Amazingly, God not only listened but he responded by changing his plans. Abraham continued bargaining until God lowered the magic number from fifty to ten righteous people.

Of course, I also noticed Abraham's attitude of deep humility in Genesis 18:27: "Now that I have been so bold as to speak to the Lord, though I am nothing but dust and ashes . . ." This attitude contrasts with the attitude we often display toward authority figures. For instance, during a recent World Cup soccer tournament, complaints about the officiating were at an all-time high. Comments like "the refs are idiots" and "the refs ruined the game" were routine. As a high school basketball player, I used to do the same thing. After clobbering an opponent with a forearm shiver and getting charged with a foul, I'd raise my hands in mock protest as if to say, "Who me? Ref, you've got to be kidding! I hardly touched the guy." In both examples the confrontation with the refs stems from an arrogance that says, "I know better than you. My opinion is superior to yours."

That's not the attitude behind this type of prayer. As Abraham confronted God, arguing and negotiating with God, he also stood humbly before God and said, "I am nothing but dust and ashes." Or, "You made me out of dust and you could turn me back to dust—or a tiny grease spot—in the next nanosecond, but I still must ask this question." Prayers of confrontation involve incredible humility and a hushed sense of wonder that I'm allowed to approach God at all. God and I aren't equal sparring partners. It's not the difference between a referee and a soccer midfielder. It's the difference between the Creator and the created; the Maker and the dust; the Potter and the pot. And yet I'm still invited by God to come and engage with God, even arguing with the living and holy God of the universe.

Moses. I knew all about Moses, but I had never noticed that he also demonstrated the practice of prayer as an argument with God. After God had led his people out of slavery in Egypt, they started wandering—very slowly—to the Promised Land. Moses was responsible for this unruly bunch of bullheaded, whiny, cantankerous people. But before they even started this long journey, God made a simple, clear promise to Moses: "I will be with you" (Exodus 3:12); "I will help you" (Exodus 4:12). But now Moses' massive family-camping expedition with a cast of thousands was starting to unravel as the whining reached epidemic proportions (see Numbers 11:4).

When Moses had heard enough, he started to argue with God: "Why have you brought this trouble on your servant? What have I done to displease you that you put the burden of all these people on me? Did I conceive all these people? Did I give them birth?" (Numbers 11:11-12). In other words, "This is your problem, God, so why aren't you taking care of *your* problem?" He went on: "Why do you tell me to carry them in my arms, as a nurse carries an infant, to the land you promised on oath to their forefathers?" (Numbers 11:12). First, Moses presented God with the evidence of God's own promises; then Moses asked God to remember and fulfill those promises. "Where can I get meat for all these people? . . . I cannot carry all these people by myself; the burden is too heavy for me. If this is how you are going to treat me, put me to death right now" (Numbers 11:13-15). In other words, Moses implied, "You aren't coming through on your end of the bargain, God. I can't handle this. I'm overwhelmed and I'm sinking fast."

I'm still amazed that God actually listened to Moses—without telling him to shut up—and then God responded to Moses. In verses 16-17 God responds like a business consultant, offering suggestions that will help Moses delegate some of his massive administrative duties. Moses addressed God, presenting his complaint to God, who is both judge and defendant. Moses made his requests, and God listened and intervened on Moses' behalf.

In this process of arguing with God, we grow closer through the confrontation. Christian counselor William Gaultiere has seen this scenario played out in his counseling sessions. "Among the Christians I work with in therapy," he claims, "it has been my experience that those who are willing to honestly wrestle with God by confronting, questioning, or even complaining to Him about the pain and injustice they experience are the ones who develop the most intimate relationship with him."[4] That's exactly what God did for Moses: God listened, engaged Moses in a real conversation and then God responded to Moses' confrontation.

The psalmist. In Psalm 10 I found another example of prayer as confrontation. This psalm begins with an urgent address to God: "Why, O Lord, do you stand far off? Why do you hide yourself in times of trouble?" (Psalm 10:1). From there he launches into a presentation of the evidence brought to God against God based on God's justice. The following verses contain these snippets of this prayer as arguing with God: "In his arrogance the wicked man hunts down the weak, who are caught in the schemes he devises. . . . His ways [i.e., the ways of wicked people who oppress the poor] are always prosperous; he is haughty and your laws are far from him; he sneers at all his enemies. . . . His victims are crushed, they collapse; they fall under his strength" (Psalm 10:2, 5, 10). Then notice how the psalmist makes a request from God, beginning in verse 12: "Arise LORD! Lift up your hand, O God. Do not forget the helpless. Why does the wicked man revile God? . . . But you, O God, do see trouble and grief. . . . The victim commits himself to you; you are the helper of the fatherless" (Psalm 10:12-14). The psalmist trusts that God will respond because he knows God's character. God is a helper of the fatherless, so he won't ignore this prayer.

Prayer as an argument with God isn't just for myself and my needs: God wants me to engage him for the sake of others as well, especially the vulnerable and oppressed. In our fast-paced, competitive lifestyle, we're sometimes tempted to view every expression of hurt as just another instance of victimization and whining. But knowing that God receives my prayers of argument, that he even trains me to confront him, I'm encouraged to come to him on behalf of the victimized. As a follower of Jesus, as someone who claims to talk to the living God, now I realize that I could never read the *New York Times* the same way. Every story of contemporary injustice urges me to engage God on behalf of the weak.

Jewish writer Elie Wiesel contends that this path of prayer is deeply rooted in a biblically shaped view of the world:

> To be a Jew means to serve God by espousing man's cause, to plead for man while recognizing his need for God. And to opt for the Creator and his creation, refusing to pit one against the other. Of course man must interrogate God, as did Abraham; articulate his anger, as did Moses; and shout his sorrows, as did Job. But only the Jew [and the Christian, I would add] opts for Abraham—who questions—and for God—who is questioned.[5]

In our prayers of confrontation we side with both God and the one who questions God. A few months ago I was reading Psalm 10 side by side with a book review that described the plight of millions of women—many of them mere children—who are lured into and then trapped in the jaws of the global sex trade. Based on the approach to God outlined in Psalm 10, I started to pray like this: *God, this global sex trade isn't right. It's a tragedy. My God, look at the children! You're a God of justice, and this doesn't look like justice. You're a God of the moral straight line, but this looks so crooked and bent. And rich pimps are getting fatter off the profit of this grubby business. It's disgusting! So, good God in heaven, do something about it. I can't accept this situation anymore. And I can't accept it because I know who you are: a God of justice for the oppressed, the Father to the fatherless.*

When I pray like this I realize that prayer isn't just an exercise in private piety or personal holiness. It connects us with the God who is the Father to the fatherless and the liberator of the oppressed.

SLAMMING OUR PRAYERS BACK TO GOD

Confronting God? Arguing with God? Hauling God to court? I'm still wrestling with the implications of this pattern for prayer. I was taught to be nice—on the playground and in my prayer times. These were some of my basic rules for civilized praying people: close your eyes, fold your hands, be respectful, think positive thoughts and say pleasant words to God. Arguing is bad because it ruptures intimacy with the Almighty. But prayer as confrontation makes my prayer life more ragged and wild. It turns some (not all, but certainly some) of my civilized prayer rules upside down. Where is this path of prayer leading me?

The biblical tradition of prayer as confrontation means that I must take my prayer life with utmost seriousness. This prayer path encourages us to grab on to God; argue with God; flail at God; ask God, "Why?" and "How long?" and "When will you wake up and do something?"; hop around because you're so bleeping mad. With the psalmist you can pray, "Arise, O LORD, in your anger; rise up against the rage of my enemies. Awake, my God; decree justice" (Psalm 7:6-7). Lean hard into God with rage or doubt, but don't come to God with pious but cold prayers that never engage your heart or the pain of this broken cosmos. God grows weary of syrupy sweet prayers that are detached and passionless.

In volleyball it's the difference between a dink shot and a spike. Dink shots are tiny shots that just barely pop over the net and fall delicately and precisely on the other side. Occasionally they score points, but in volleyball the dink shot isn't your basic weapon. Usually you'll score with a spike shot. You have to slam the ball back to the other side. So in my life of prayer, God sometimes says, "Go ahead and spike it back to me. I don't want an unending litany of dink shots. Slam it to me. I can take it. If you feel uncomfortable, I'll even warm you up with some choice words. Try Psalm 7 or Psalm 10 or Psalm 44. Or get mentored by a few of my favorite characters: Moses and Abraham and Jeremiah. You might even change my mind. But just go ahead and give it your best shot."

I'm still shocked by this pattern for prayer, but based on these Bible passages—and so many more—I'm not sure how else to say it. Yes, I must acknowledge that God is sovereign and I'm not. God is wise and I'm not. God's timing can be so different than mine. God may allow suffering for a greater purpose and to create greater beauty in us and through us. But confrontational prayer reminds me to keep engaging God, wrestling with God and passionately pursuing God.

THE God WHO PASSIONATELY PURSUES ME

Prayer involves my passionate pursuit of and engagement with God. But more than anything, I'm learning that prayer ushers me into God's passionate pursuit of me. The biblical tradition of arguing with God tells me something profound and wonderful about the gospel, the good news of what Christ has done for us and in us. I've often had the impression that the essence of Christian spirituality is what I do for God or how well I behave for God. So I try hard to be clean, to act nice, to be kinder and less angry. I may serve on a committee or dress up for church or dress down for church. And if I can say a few pious prayers with the right words, I hope that it's good enough to please God.

But the gospel turns all of this on its head. It constantly tells me, "Look how much the Father loves you! He is a jealous God who wants your heart. He is a passionate God who has fought for you. Now, because he has set you free, because he died for you when you wandered away from him, love and obey him with your whole heart." God wants me. God wants my heart, my fully engaged heart, even when it's brimming with a potent brew of anger and doubt and pain.

How much did God love me and pursue me? I keep coming back to what Jesus did for us on the cross. Jesus, God the Son, cries out to God the Father, "*Eloi, Eloi, lama sabachthani,*" or "My God, my God, why have you forsaken me?" (Mark 15:34, emphasis in original). It's a prayer of confrontation from Jesus, God the Son, to God the Father. "Father, where are you?" he cried out. If I accept the Christian story, it leads me to a startling conclusion: Jesus was and is God in human flesh, which means that God himself has stepped into my shoes, taking my place, standing in solidarity with all of us in our pain, confusion, anger and sense of abandonment. God knows all the feelings and pain behind our prayers of confrontation.

And God doesn't just receive this kind of prayer; God has made this kind of prayer.

I found this realization absolutely stunning. God not only allows us to argue with him, but God knows from personal experience how to argue with God. On the cross, God confronted God, and yet at the same time, God the Son trusted and submitted to God the Father. Then God allows us to argue with him.

How do I grasp this? How do I grasp the depths God has gone to show us his love, his deep identification and solidarity with human beings? A number of years ago someone wrote an imaginary scenario to reflect how God has suffered with us and for us. I liked it when I read it twenty years ago, but it needed some updating. So a while ago I took the little parable and adapted it. My new version goes like this:

> At the end of time, billions of people were scattered on a great plain before God's throne. Most shrank back from the brilliant light before them. But some groups near the front talked heatedly—not with cringing shame, but with rage.
>
> "Can God judge us? How can he know about suffering?" snapped a young woman from Pakistan who had spent sixteen hours a day making soccer balls. An elderly woman from Ohio with a hunched back murmured, "I was so alone. Everyone abandoned me. And where were you, God?" A tenth-grade girl lowered her eyes and said, "Why, God? Why did you allow him to abuse me? It ruined my life, God! No, you ruined my life!" A ragged street child from Rio de Janeiro groaned, "The hunger! I was always so hungry. Every day I scrounged through hotel dumpsters while the tourists ate like kings. Why?"
>
> Far out across the plain, there were hundreds of such groups. Each had a complaint against God for the suffering he had permitted in his world. God was lucky: he lived in heaven where everything was safe and sweet. What did God know of human pain and agony? They all agreed: God leads a sheltered life.
>
> So they decided to confront God. They proceeded to select a group of people who had suffered the most: a Cuban poet tortured for more than twenty years in a damp cell; a refugee from Darfur whose hands had been chopped off; a hungry crack baby from Chicago; and a teenage orphan from Iraq. In the center of

> the plain they consulted with each other. At last they were ready to present their argument to God against God.
>
> In order to qualify to judge others, God must endure human anguish. So they sentenced God to live on the earth as a human being. "Let him be born a wandering, poor refugee," they shouted. "Let the legitimacy of his birth be doubted. Give him a demanding job. Let him be betrayed by his closest friends. Let him face charges, be tried by a prejudiced jury and convicted by a cowardly judge. At the last, let him be tortured and whipped, and then let God die naked and alone, a victim of abuse and injustice."
>
> As each leader announced his portion of the sentence, loud murmurs of approval went up from the throng of people assembled. And when the refugee from Darfur had finished pronouncing the sentence, there was a long silence. No one uttered another word. No one moved. Everyone knew that God had already served his sentence.[6]

As I continue to journey down the path of prayer as confrontation, based on the words of the Bible and my Jesus-following Jewish friends, God seems to tell me, "Go ahead: slam it back to me. Do you feel abandoned or confused? Slam it back to me. Are you outraged by the injustices of the world? Slam it back it to me. Are you angry and hurt? Slam it back to me. Do you, a pile of dust and ashes, feel like picking a fight with the Almighty? Slam it back to me. Do you feel that I'm doing a lousy job of running the world or your life? Slam it back to me. Go ahead and give me your best shot. Hit your prayers right into my face. I can take it. I already took it when my Son died on the cross."

So there will be days when I tell God, "I love you, Lord, I love you but I'm mad and confused." I'm convinced that God would rather have a good argument than a cold shoulder. But I'm also convinced that every prayer I slam back at God hits a face of warm, fatherly love. And that face of love will just keep returning love.

7

PRAYER AS A LONG, SLOW JOURNEY

Last August my seventeen-year-old son was supposed to catch a flight from Chicago to Long Island at 4:00 p.m. Due to storms near the East Coast, at 8:00 p.m. the plane remained stuck at Midway Airport. By 9:00 p.m. the airline website claimed that the flight had left Chicago—without my son. In the confusion I called the Midway police department, which informed me that the flight was still waiting at the gate. At 2:00 the next morning, with the plane still stalled at Midway, I reached an agent for my son's airline. Unfortunately (and pathetically), I lost my temper and started ranting at the young woman, demanding free flights, free meals and beverages, and a big, fat apology. I used words like "horrible," "inefficient" and "incompetent." Embarrassed by his father's pushiness, my son took the phone from her and told me, "Gee, Dad, cut her some slack; everyone's doing the best they can here." Finally, at 4:00 a.m., the flight left Midway Airport, arriving on Long Island more than twelve hours behind schedule.

A few days later I received an e-mail from a friend named Diane who runs a ministry in Sudan. She asked us to pray about a critical situation: the unusually heavy rains in the Upper Nile had displaced thousands of families. For months, flights in and out of Sudan would be canceled. Diane wrote, "We have had difficulty taking medicine and basic supplies into Sudan. Children are having difficulty getting to school. We can't get relief supplies in to people who are destitute due to the flooding." This wasn't just a twelve-hour wait for one child; this was an agonizing season of waiting for thousands of people, one that could last up to eighteen months.

That certainly put my "horrible" waiting experience in perspective. And it certainly caused me to ponder some uncomfortable questions about my approach to life: Why is it so hard for me to wait? Why am I so impatient? Why do I want what I want right now?

PATIENCE: THE MISSING DIMENSION

After spending thirty-five years deepening my prayer life and then helping others to pray too, I'm convinced that a healthy prayer life requires large doses of patience. But sadly, our impatient approach to life often undermines our efforts to pray.

This pattern of prayerlessness often follows a well-worn path: first, we need something. Someone is hurting and we want help. We've tried to fix it ourselves, but we can't, so when it gets intolerable, we come to God and say, "Lord, I just can't take any more of this. Change this situation before it swallows me alive."

Then God should respond and fix the problem. Throughout history God "rescues and he saves; he performs signs and wonders in the heavens and on the earth" (Daniel 6:27). So God should do stuff for us; that's his job.

Of course, our problem is usually simple: we're in a hurry, but God isn't. God works slowly (at least it seems that way to us). We want it now, but God takes his own sweet time puttering around up there doing who knows what. With all due respect, you'd think God could process those requests more efficiently. Naturally, God's puttering pattern makes us discouraged. Perhaps we even stop praying altogether. "What's the point?" we say. "If it takes that long to get a response, why do I even pray?"

Unfortunately, this scenario is missing one critical dimension to our prayer life. It's not a huge secret because this phrase is practically plastered all over the pages of the Bible: *Wait on the Lord.* The Psalms often remind us to wait on the Lord: "I waited patiently for the LORD; he turned to me and heard my cry" (Psalm 40:1); "Be still before the LORD and wait patiently for him" (Psalm 37:7); "I wait for the LORD, my soul waits, and in his word I put my hope" (Psalm 130:5). The prophet Isaiah declared, "Blessed are all who wait for him!" (Isaiah 30:18). Jeremiah also claimed that "it is good to wait quietly for the salvation of the LORD" (Lamentations 3:26). And the New Testament writer James tells us, "Be patient, then, brothers. . . . See how the farmer waits" (James 5:7). Based on this clear biblical teaching, it's little surprise that the philosopher Simone Weil would contend that "waiting patiently in expectation is the foundation of the spiritual life."[1]

Without this dimension of patience or waiting on the Lord, we develop the wrong assumption about prayer: we think that prayer is primarily about getting things from God—right now!—rather than primarily about being with God. We assume prayer implies that God must change our circumstances right now, when prayer really implies that God needs to change us. We neglect the truth that prayer ushers us into God-time, a broad and spacious land where things move slowly but perfectly. In particular, waiting-on-the-Lord prayer changes the rhythm in our souls; it adjusts us to God's timetable, not the other way around. As a result, as we pray, as we spend time in God's presence, we start moving at the speed of God. On a practical level this changes us by training us in the art of love, because without patience, we'll never learn to love well. Prayer bends our souls to the speed of God's loving purposes for us, for our loved ones and for the whole earth. We can't pray well without having our spiritual clocks adjusted to God-time.

OUR PUSHY, IMPATIENT LIFESTYLE

Unfortunately, we usually don't want our lives bent to fit with God-time. We're perfectly adjusted to our culture's time, and as a result the beauty and strength of patience has diminished. In his book *Patience: How We Wait upon the World,* David Baily Harned argues that there are two pervasive assumptions of our age that have caused our patience to atrophy. First, we're firmly convinced that waiting and the need for patience are purely accidental. In other words, we shouldn't have to wait. A few months ago I went to McDonald's to order a quick lunch for my son and me. After I received my order, I noticed that the cash register was flashing the total price and the total time it took to fulfill our order: 49 seconds. Imagine that: two sandwiches, two orders of fries, chicken McNuggets and two ice cream cones—*with sprinkles!*—in 11 seconds less than a minute. Clearly McDonald's assumes that waiting should be accidental to my life. No wonder God's sense of timing irks us. Our whole society has subscribed to an unwritten code: waiting is an abnormal and even obscene party crasher in our lives. Let's banish it with 49-second meals.

Second, most of us also assume that "real life" involves getting things done, checking off items on my to-do list and working efficiently. In contrast, we view waiting as a listless, passive, unproductive non-activity. Waiting is beyond the pale of real life. For instance, who wants to be a "patient"? Hospital patients don't do anything; they just take up a bed, rack up a huge bill, and let doctors and nurses "perform" procedures on them. Thus, according to Harned, "We assume that we are most fully human when we are in control, actors and not acted upon, subjects rather than objects. What matters is what we accomplish, not what we are given."[2]

As a result of our waiting-revulsion, we don't pray, or at least we don't pray well. If praying well means immersing our lives in God-time, then our cultural assumptions about waiting shrivel our prayer lives. Clearly, in terms of timing God and I are not on the same page. Perhaps God will change his mind or his sense of timing (see Genesis 18:16-33 and Exodus 32:9-14). But what if that doesn't happen? How do I amend my prayer life to the reality of God-time?

A LONG, SLOW JOURNEY FORWARD

We can begin by reading the Bible for what it is: a long, slow journey that constantly calls for patience. The Bible is filled with examples of waiting. Noah waited for the floodwaters to recede (see Genesis 8:10-12). Abraham and Sarah waited for the child of the promise (see Genesis 12–21). Their grandson Jacob worked for his crooked uncle Laban for seven years so he could marry Laban's beautiful daughter Rachel. After Laban substituted his other daughter, Leah, on the wedding night, Jacob waited seven more years to win his true love, Rachel (Genesis 29:15-30). For fourteen years he loved Rachel and waited for her and pined with desire for her. I get annoyed when I'm forced to wait an extra five seconds at a stoplight.

Then God called Joseph to a special destiny, but in God-time it took years to fulfill, and it required a twisty path of abandonment, betrayal, imprisonment and more abandonment before the special destiny was fulfilled (Genesis 37; 39–43). The children of Israel waited as slaves in Egypt for hundreds of years (Exodus 2:23). Finally God miraculously delivered them, but then they proceeded to wander in the desert yet another forty years.

You'd think that those desert wanderings would force them to adjust to God's time; unfortunately, it just perfected them in the art of kvetching. *Kvetch* is a Yiddish word that means "to complain."[3] It's usually a clear indicator that we haven't adjusted our prayer life to God's timetable. A contemporary kvetch might sound like this: "Oy, vei! This is ridiculous. The Department of Motor Vehicles runs things better than you! Sure, Lord God, you can make us wait, but we'll do our part by not liking it." Throughout their history, God's people were forced to wait, but they kept kvetching.

The Old Testament prophets also waited. After the last words from the Old Testament prophets, God instituted a deep silence of four hundred years between the two testaments. To gain perspective on God-time, let me ask this: Where were you in the year 1610? Do you remember? Do you know anyone who does? Finally, after this four-hundred-year pause, God fulfilled his promises and came in human flesh as Jesus, our Immanuel. But even Jesus, God-in-the-flesh, had to wait: patiently growing up, memorizing Scripture, obeying his parents, mastering the craft of carpentry, waiting for his public ministry to begin. After his death and resurrection, the early church had to wait for the coming of the Holy Spirit.

Most of us can relate to this biblical story line because we, too, find ourselves in waiting places. After nearly twenty years of a pain-filled marriage, my friend Jack is waiting for healing in his relationship with his wife, but it won't come overnight. They're plodding through painful issues in their marital counseling, but their problems won't get unraveled quickly. My friend Susie is waiting for her health to return after a wicked case of breast cancer. She's cancer-free now, but the doctors say it could take a few years for her body to spring back to full health. My friend Scott is waiting for healing in his soul. He's in the grip of a strong addiction, but the root issues of his addiction are deep and tangled inside his soul. By pursuing health, Scott has enlisted in a long battle.

THE WORLD'S BIGGEST WAITER

The biblical story requires patience of almost everyone, but the biggest waiter is God. If you think you have to be patient, imagine how God feels about us? And yet God waits for us with great joy! Time and again the Bible declares that God is patient with his us. God suffers long with us. "The LORD, the LORD, the compassionate and gracious God, slow to anger, abounding in love and faithfulness" (Exodus 34:6). The patience of God is the superglue that holds the Bible's plot together.

Some people are appalled when they read the Bible and discover that God gets angry with human beings. Seemingly out of nowhere, God blows up and unleashes plagues or an earthquake or a flood. But we forget the timetable: in most cases God patiently endured dysfunctional, screwed-up, destructive human behavior for decades, centuries and sometimes even millennia before stepping in and saying, "Okay, that's enough. Someone has to stop this behavior and clean up the mess."

In the New Testament, no one deserved more impatience than the apostle Paul. He was a first-class religious jerk—angry, smug, judgmental and violent. And yet Paul would say, "Christ Jesus came into the world to save sinners—of whom I am the worst. But for that very reason I was shown mercy so that in me, the worst of sinners, Christ Jesus might display his unlimited patience as an example for those who would believe on him" (1 Timothy 1:15-16).

Most of the "big words" in the Christian story are tied to the patience of God, who is for us in Christ Jesus. *Creation* means that God, unlike the gods or goddesses in some creation myths, doesn't destroy the world over and over again. Actually, right now Jesus himself is patiently holding the world together (Colossians 1:16-17). *Incarnation* means that God is patient with human flesh and human bodies because he became flesh for us. *Atonement* means that God is patient even when God should have turned his face away from us. On the cross Jesus died for us, in our place.

Hitting the Pause Button

Immersing ourselves in the Bible's view of patience will change our prayer lives. While impatience strangles the roots of prayer before it sprouts, waiting on God provides the right soil for cultivating prayer. Without patience, everything in our lives becomes a frantic, loud, urgent "now": have it now, do it now, get it now, experience fulfillment now, understand it now, get it done now, relieve the pain now. There's no time to wait. There's no time to be sick and recover. There's no time to rebuild broken things. There's no time for the tension of the "not yet." Everything smears into a quest for spiritual, emotional and relational 49-second happy meals.

We can't hit the pause button and give God space to work. So we fill in the pause with our ceaseless activity and pushy demands. But if everything depends on us, if we don't believe that we have a Father who loves us and who has perfect timing for us and our loved ones, then why even pray? It's unnecessary. Instead, we'll live grasping, demanding, impatient lives that resent the party crasher of waiting.

But God-time, patient time, waiting-on-the-Lord time, allows a pause between the request to God and the response from God. Pause time is a rich time. The pause isn't empty, nothing-is-happening time; it's pregnant with meaning and activity because God is active and alert, steering us and refining us. Referring to the forty-year wait given to the children of Israel, Japanese scholar Kosuke Koyama commented: "Forty years for one lesson! How slow and how patient! No university can run on that basis. . . . I find that God goes 'slowly' in his educational process with man. . . . Isn't this a rather slow and costly way for God to let his people know the covenant relationship between God and man?"[4] Well, yes, it is slow and costly, not to mention horribly inefficient. But God's best lessons are slow lessons.

True prayer means that I can hit the pause button and let go, trusting the Lord to fill the gaps. I can even enjoy the waiting season. In her beautiful article titled "Fall from Grace: How Modern Life Has Made Waiting a Desperate Act," the poet Noelle Oxenhandler tells the story of Jacques Lusseyran, a blind Frenchman who joined the Nazi resistance movement. Oxenhandler comments: "What impressed me as much as his heroic activity was the pause that preceded it. For weeks he simply absorbed the reality of Paris under the Occupation—a strange emptiness in the streets, except for the certain neighborhoods that swarmed with Nazi soldiers." After a prolonged illness, Lusseyran decided to join the resistance. Still, despite the sense of urgency, he had to do one thing before engaging the Nazis: he took dancing lessons. So he hit the pause button and learned basic dance steps, the waltz and then swing. "When you had whirled a pack of girls at arms length for five or six hours . . . you were dead beat. But still you had driven off the devils."[5]

Dancing while the Nazis roamed the streets? Whirling girls during wartime? What a waste of time! Or was it? Perhaps the pause prepared Lusseyran for the battle ahead. Perhaps he could wait because he trusted, deep down, in the eventual victory of good over evil, not his frantic activity. I don't know his story, but I do see him as a role model for my prayer life. We trust in the risen Christ, who is "making everything new" (Revelation 21:5). Clearly, God has called me to bring cold water to the thirsty, to clothe the naked, to offer Christ to the soul-famished. God calls me to act in the midst of my own crises and needs. But does everything depend on my action? What do I do when God ushers me into God-time? Do I rail against it? Do I start moving at hyperspeed? Can I keep praying and dancing even when I'm waiting on the Lord? Do I believe that God will "bring all things in heaven and on earth together under one head, even Christ" (Ephesians 1:10)? Can I rest and whirl in God-time?

Waiting on God enables me to trust God's good plans for my life, even when I don't understand (or agree with) his timing for my life. Thus, patience is the soil of true prayer. In another way, patiently waiting on God is a prayer in itself. By waiting on God, by accepting and even enjoying the pauses of life, I am saying, "God, you are big enough, wise enough, good enough to lead me and guide my life."

How does prayer change us? How do we enter this spacious and gracious land of God's patience? How do I walk with God at the speed of love? Prayer as a long, slow journey will move me to pray through suffering, to pray for "slow people" and to pray in self-acceptance.

PRAYING THROUGH OUR SUFFERING

Living and praying in God-time enables me to "suffer well." Waiting is difficult; sometimes it's even agonizing. We wait for healing to come. We wait for a wayward child to find his way. We wait for someone to return our love. We wait to rebuild broken lives and communities and institutions. We wait for the loneliness to end. We cry out, "How long must I wait, Lord?"

Not all of this is just kvetching. There is a legitimate place to express our agony, for followers of Jesus aren't Stoics. Stoicism was the tradition in the West that prized patience above all the other virtues. Regarding the endless turmoil of impatient anger, the Stoic philosopher Seneca wrote, "Shall we not summon ourselves to patience when it promises so great a reward, the unmoved serenity of a happy mind?"

The early church leaders shared the Stoic value of patience, but they rejected the Stoic indifference to God's world. Stoicism valued self-sufficiency; Christianity valued interdependent, redemptive love. Stoicism urged people to avoid real love because it hurts too much; Christianity pursued a love that endures through suffering. Stoics neatly divided the world into the worthy/wise and the unworthy/foolish; Christians embraced everyone because God the Father showers his love on the just and the unjust.[6]

We are not Stoics. We weep; we groan; we rail; we hurt; we love. But we also live in the shadow of the cross and resurrection of Jesus, so our patience glimmers with hope and even joy. The good news we share in and through Jesus means that ultimately waiting won't diminish us. Instead, waiting creates room in us; it expands us.

In the fourth century the brilliant theologian Augustine noted the profound way that waiting enlarges rather than contracts our soul: "The entire Christian life is an exercise in holy desire. You do not see what you long for, but the very act of desiring prepares you, so that when he comes you may see and be utterly satisfied." Then he used the following analogy: imagine you have a large bucket of water that must be poured into a wineskin. You must first stretch the wineskin so it can hold all the water. The stretching increases the wineskin's capacity to hold more water. Augustine claimed that God uses waiting to increase our capacity to hold him: "Simply by making us wait he increases our desire, which in turn enlarges the capacity of our soul, making it able to receive what is to be given to us."[7]

Waiting is God's good work in us. Waiting is pregnant with genesis power. When I preached a sermon on waiting, a Ph.D. student approached me and asked a simple question: "That was all good theory, but can you tell me a story of when you had to wait for something?" So I told her the story of my desire to get a book published. Fifteen years earlier I'd felt (at least I thought I'd felt) a call from God to write a book. So for fifteen years I worked on a book that went through numerous revisions before an editor wanted to publish it. Unfortunately, that company was purchased by a larger company, and my book went down the drain. Then a few years later another major publisher bought the book, and we even had a signed contract before they reneged on the deal. I was angry and crushed. I felt like a loser and I didn't want to write again.

The book idea hibernated in my computer for a year until my friend David said, "Matt, you have to get that book out there." That idea made me sick. "David," I said, "thanks, but that book idea is dead; I've grieved and I just want to move on." A year later David approached me again about the book. "Okay," I said, "go ahead and send it in, but I'm not expecting anything." A year and a half later the book was finally published.

This wasn't exactly a life-or-death struggle, but I did learn a profound lesson. When the first publisher almost bought the book, I wasn't ready to publish the book. When the second publisher reneged on the contract, I still wasn't ready. My life didn't match the content in the book. In other words, I was living like a hypocrite. So God in his infinite patience and wisdom and mercy kept thwarting my desire to publish a book. He needed to deepen my soul. During the waiting time, the pause time, that's exactly what God did in my soul. He prepared my heart by humbling me, stripping me of arrogance and hypocrisy. He made me real.

PRAYING FOR "SLOW PEOPLE"

When we wait on God, we learn the art of love. Specifically, we learn to pray for "slow people." Harned contends, "Wherever patience is absent, love sours, leaving no more than a dreadful parody of itself."[8] When I wait on God, it teaches me and trains me to move at the speed of love. Koyama reminds us that "God walks 'slowly' because he is love. . . . Love has its speed. It is an inner speed. It is a spiritual speed. It is a different kind of speed from the technological speed to which we are accustomed. It is a 'slow' yet it is lord over all other speeds since it is the speed of love."[9]

Have you ever noticed that people make us impatient? They—

people, that is—are so annoying because they are notoriously slow. I've discovered two categories of slow people:

1. Regular slow people

2. Really slow people

The regular slow people include everyone—except me, of course. Regular slow people just aren't as quick as we'd like them to be. They don't change as fast as us. They don't meet our expectations for speedy transformation. If you're married, your spouse is probably too slow for you. Friends can be slow. Parents or children are known for their slowness. Churches can move slowly. Come to think of it, I'm pretty darn slow too. Gosh, from God's viewpoint, I'm incredibly slow.

Really slow people make regular slow people look like cheetahs. They range across the life span, from the unborn (they hardly move at all, except occasionally when they kick you) to the very old. They move slowly. Some of them think slowly. Some of them heal slowly. Some of them suffer from lifelong physical or mental disabilities. Being with them takes extra time and patience. We're tempted to pick up our pace and move on without them. They're just too darn slow for "fast folk" like us.

But once we get on God-time, once we start waiting on God, once we see and feel the slowness of God's pace in the world, once I realize how slow I move, I can start loving those really slow people. We don't just tolerate them; we see that they are a gift to us and to our community. They are the "weaker members" that actually hold our community together. In a way, we need them more than they need us (see 1 Corinthians 12:22-25). Really slow people serve as our mentors in adjusting to God's time. They evangelize us by reminding us of the good news of Jesus' incredible patience toward us. Just watching them, loving them, embracing them can teach us to pray.

Throughout the New Testament, followers of Jesus are urged to "be patient" with one another, as in 1 Thessalonians 5:14. The Greek word used here for patience is *makrothumia,* which comes from *makros,* or "long," and *thumos,* or "anger." Thus, patience means that it takes a long time to get angry, or that we are long-suffering. It doesn't mean that we never get angry; it just means that, like God, we have a long fuse rather than a short fuse.[10]

Patience is the cartilage of Christian community: without patience we just grate on each other like bone against bone. Patience makes us soft; it helps us endure one another. As we pray for people, as we adjust to God's timetable for life, we can wait for others no matter how slow they may seem to us. We give others the gift of space and time.

PRAYING IN SELF-ACCEPTANCE

It's hard to be patient with myself. I can act like one screwed-up human being. On the other hand, I'm also a glorious creature made in the image of God, tarnished by sin but being remade in the glorious image of Jesus Christ. But this process of remaking takes time. There's always a tension between what I am right now and what I will be. The tension, the gap (okay, sometimes it's a chasm) between where I am and where I should be fosters an impatient rejection of myself—perhaps even a violent self-hatred.

How do I live with myself as I wait for God to finish the process of redemption in my life? How do I avoid self-hatred or impatience toward my own spiritual growth? By praying in a spirit of self-acceptance. In the wise words of Romano Guardini, "Patience with oneself—of course not carelessness or weakness, but the sense of reality—this is the foundation of all progress."[11] Of course, as we yearn for our full redemption, we deal honestly with the sin in our lives, regularly repenting before God and confessing our sin before our brothers and sisters in Christ (see James 5:16). But an impatient, pushy, pressurized, you-better-stop-sinning-and-grow-up-in-Christ-right-now approach to spirituality just doesn't work.

Believe me, I've tried this approach for years, and it never helped. I thought that if I could just inject a little more shame and self-hatred into my life, I would finally grow up and start acting more like Jesus. But these forms of impatience with myself merely feed the underlying problem: a focus on myself. Growth occurs and continues when we stop depending on ourselves and we start relying on God. That's the gospel. God undermines all of our little self-redemption projects, leaving us with one and only one hope: Jesus. And then he covers us with the righteousness of Christ and fills us with the power of his Spirit.

Over the past few years this has been one of the most profound lessons of my life. It's easy to look back with regret (i.e., "Why did I make so many stupid mistakes? Why didn't I learn those lessons faster? How could I have been so dense?"). It's also easy to look forward with dread (i.e., "I have so far to go. I'm still not the person I want to be. What if I make the same mistakes again?"). Both self-regret and dread just fuel hatred toward self, but the gospel obliterates both. Both regret and dread—and every other form of self-impatience—are useless to the spiritual journey. Patience with ourselves on a spiritual journey with Christ will propel us forward.

THE STRENGTH OF PATIENCE

In the midst of our waiting-on-God times, we're tempted to throw up our hands and scream, "Forget it, God! I can't stand it anymore. I can't wait any longer." But prayer changes us. It changes our spiritual geography, ushering us into the broad and spacious and gracious geography of God. It's the space where things happen slowly but perfectly according to God's good timing for our lives.

And patience isn't a weak, passive, listless virtue. Prayer as a long, slow journey demands great strength, and it produces great love. As Romano Guardini wrote, "Only the strong man can exercise living patience, can take upon himself again and again the things that are; only he can always begin anew. Patience without strength is mere passivity, dull acceptance, growing accustomed to being a mere thing. Love, too, belongs to patience—love of life. For living things grow slowly, take their time, and have many twists and turns. . . . He who does not love life has no patience with it."[12]

8

PRAYER AS A DANGEROUS ACTIVITY

In the film *Jumanji,* two orphan children move in with their aunt in a mysterious old house. After a few days the children wander up to the attic, where they find a stack of dust-covered board games. They pull Jumanji off the pile, and as they move the game pieces around the board, strange things start to happen: gigantic mosquitoes dive at their heads, a herd of monkeys takes over the kitchen, and a huge lion tries to maul them. Apparently this isn't just an innocent, boring kids' game. By opening the box, they've unleashed something powerful and dangerous as they embark on the adventure of a lifetime.

In one sense, prayer is like playing Jumanji. Certainly prayer in Jesus' name isn't magic, and it's not a child's game. We won't see wild monkeys and untamed lions. But when we pray, we'll meet something even wilder—the alive, free, risen and exalted Jesus himself. So when we pray in Christ's name, we'll always get much more than we bargained for.

In other words, if prayer came in a box, we should slap a big, bright, bold label on it:

Warning! Danger!
The contents of this box are unpredictable and explosive.
You may lose control of your life as you know it.
Open with extreme care!

Most of us don't think of prayer as a dangerous activity. I was raised on wonderful hymns like "Sweet Hour of Prayer," which reminded me that prayer "draws me from a world of care." Prayer is sweet. Prayer vaccinates us against danger. If prayer were a board game, it would be a nice game with clear rules designed by a predictable God who exists to help me get my little game piece safely around the board.

Yes, God is kind and gentle, and prayer can be sweet. However, when we pray, we also open our lives to the presence of the most powerful Person in the universe. And he's good, but he's not tame. God is utterly undomesticated and at times incomprehensible. So when we pray, we lose our tight grip on controlling the spiritual journey. When we open the "God-box," we always get more than we expected—more joy, more love, more danger, more adventure, more suffering and more holiness. And prayer doesn't draw us from a world of care; as we join with Jesus, he calls us (and sometimes drags us) back into a world of care, danger and brokenness.

Invocation: Opening the God-Box

The early Christians had a special word for opening the God-box: they called it the prayer of invocation. When we invoke something or someone, we call upon a presence that is more powerful than us. Of course, Christians invoke the presence of Jesus Christ. One of the oldest recorded liturgical prayers (a prayer used in a public worship service) is the simple invocation "Come, Lord Jesus." It is rooted in the New Testament (see 1 Corinthians 16:22; Revelation 22:20) and an early Christian document called *The Didache*.

Again, it wasn't magic, but when they prayed, "Come, Lord Jesus," those ancient Christ-followers expected that Jesus would show up. And when the real Jesus showed up, "stuff" happened. Today we might say "all hell broke loose." But it wasn't hell; it was the kingdom of God crashing into our world. In the Gospels, when Jesus showed up, he tossed demons around, turned fishermen into fishers of men, liberated the oppressed, exasperated religious leaders, healed desperately sick people and generally turned the world upside down. And then he empowered and sent his followers to do the same stuff. In other words, once you invoke Jesus, you can't control the results. He's free, and you won't keep Jesus in the box.

Last year some people invoked God for me, unleashing the power of Jesus on my life. I was at a difficult crossroads, so I asked Jesus for a "little help." At the same time, out of the blue, two unrelated people told me about "visions" that God had given them for my life. One happened during the Eucharist at my daughter's Anglican church. The pastor stepped out of line, put his hand on my forehead and said, "The Lord told me that your life is ready to turn into a lush and beautiful garden. Others will be blessed by the garden in your heart." A few days later a friend I hadn't heard from in years sent me a one-sentence e-mail: "The Lord told me that he will do great things in your life and through your life."

Everything seemed to be converging in my life. Jesus was appearing with power and hope and new life. I would be blessed, and I would be a blessing to others. I felt so special . . . until "all hell broke loose." In the next six months, life as I knew it shattered. God unearthed some deep roots of sin and brokenness in my heart. I kept invoking Jesus' presence, primarily asking him to make my life better. "Jesus, would you show up and take the pain away?" When I thought God had finally dug up the last of it, he was merely pausing, like a sweaty farmer wiping his brow, getting ready to plunge his shovel into the ground again, digging up more diseased roots.

I finally told God, "So this is the lush garden you promised? This is *not* what I was promised! I was expecting a nice God who had a wonderful plan for my life." But that's the problem: once you invoke Jesus, once you open your life to him, once you say that you want him to change you and pour his life through you, it's notoriously difficult to close the box and "un-invoke" him. He's always faithful to his promises, but he will fulfill those promises on his terms and in his timing, not ours. In other words, he'll always come and take us where we need to go, but the journey is rarely predictable, smooth or safe. Indeed, prayer is a dangerous activity.

C. S. Lewis once said that opening our lives to Christ is akin to visiting the dentist. Lewis claimed that as a child he tried to avoid dentists even when he was in pain. Dentists will cure the pain, Lewis said, but they won't stop there: they keep fiddling with all the other teeth. They insist on fixing everything, not just your one sore tooth. According to Lewis, Jesus acts the same way. We invoke the presence of Jesus so he can help us with one particular problem or sin or request, but he won't stop with that. "That may be all you asked; but if once you call Him in, He will give you the full treatment."[1] So every time we pray in Jesus' name, we're opening our lives to the wild lover of our souls who wants to give us "the full treatment."

God not only wants to give us the full treatment to bless us; he also wants to bless the world through us. When my friends told me that my life would be a lush garden, and then God started digging up diseased roots, I thought God's full treatment was way too severe. But now as I'm getting through this growing season, I'm starting to see the fruit. God is turning my heart into a lush garden. He has been purifying my heart—not only for my sake, but in order to make my life a blessing to others around me.

THE BIBLE'S STORY OF PRAYING DANGEROUSLY

Of course, I wasn't the first human being to encounter the dangerous nature of prayer. The biblical story abounds with men and women who called on God, who invoked his name, only to discover that God is much wilder than they ever imagined. Like us, they often had to relinquish control of their lives and let the utterly free and wild God lead them.

Certainly Abraham learned the power of invoking the name of the living God. In a way, God always invokes or calls out to us first, and then we must decide if we will return the call. So though Abraham didn't possess any qualifications, God called him and offered him an amazing set of promises:

> I will make you into a great nation
>   and I will bless you;
> I will make your name great,
>   and you will be a blessing.
> I will bless those who bless you,
>   and whoever curses you I will curse;
> and all peoples on earth
>   will be blessed through you. (Genesis 12:2-3)

The promises are simply staggering in breadth and depth. The promises were twofold: God wanted to bless Abraham, and then God promised to bless the world through Abraham's life. Would Abraham respond to God's call by calling upon the name of the Lord? Would Abraham decide to invoke the living God, receiving the promises and walking by faith? Or would he decide to keep the box closed, stay away from God and go his own way? The Bible tells us later in the story that he "called on the name of the LORD" (Genesis 13:4). By invoking God's name, Abraham started a wild, unpredictable journey with an entirely undomesticated God. Abraham wasn't in control anymore; the utterly free and wild God was leading him through the desert, through dangers and trials, through laughter and tears, through unchartable paths, until his people would arrive in the Promised Land. But none of it happened the way Abraham had imagined.

In his brilliant chapter on Abraham, appropriately titled "The Journey in the Dark," Thomas Cahill vividly describes Abraham's wild ride after invoking the presence of God in Genesis 12:

> So *wayyelekh Avram* ("Avram went")—two of the boldest words in all literature. They signal a complete departure from everything that has gone before in the long evolution of culture and sensibility. Out of Sumer, civilized repository of the predictable, comes a man who does not know where he is going but goes forth into the unknown wilderness under the prompting of his

> god. Out of Mesopotamia, home of the canny, self-serving merchants who use their gods to ensure prosperity and favor, comes a wealthy caravan with no material goal. Out of ancient humanity, which from its dim beginnings of its consciousness has read its eternal verities in the stars, comes a party traveling with no known compass. In most of Africa and Europe . . . [people] would have laughed at Abram's madness."[2]

When Abraham invoked the presence of the Lord, he started walking with God into an unknown wilderness. But Abraham's life and legacy would bless the world in ways that he had never imagined. Through Abraham, God gave us the exodus, the Law, the prophets, the promises of the kingdom, the presence of Jesus and the hope of resurrection. Even today, followers of Jesus are still also called "children of Abraham" (Galatians 3:7). So Abraham could rewrite that old hymn to say, "Sweet hour of prayer, sweet hour of prayer, that draws me from a world of care, and then plunges me back into that same world of care so God can bless the world through me."

PRAYING DANGEROUSLY WITH JESUS

In perfect harmony with his Father, God the Son also blesses us so we can be a blessing to others. And in line with Abraham, those who invoke the name of Jesus discover that prayer is a dangerous activity. For the Christian, the essence of prayer is being with Jesus. Sometimes being with Jesus feels sweet and safe, but at other times prayer may feel like we've been strapped into a Manhattan taxi with a highly skilled but slightly crazy cab driver. The cabbie will deliver you to the promised destination, but he may make some high-speed twists, hair-raising turns and skull-jarring bumps that will leave you gasping for air. At times your job is simply to hang on. Obviously this analogy has its flaws, but when you invoke Jesus, you're in for the ride of your life.

Every time I read the Gospels, I feel sorry for the disciples. They had such a nice, normal, predictable, controllable life—until Jesus showed up. After Jesus called them to himself and after they invoked his name, all hell broke loose—literally: their first assignment involved casting out demons (see Mark 3:14-15). On another occasion we're told that Jesus "*made* his disciples get into the boat and go on ahead of him to Bethsaida" (Mark 6:45, emphasis added). Apparently they didn't want to go, because the Greek word *anagkadzo* means "to force or compel." As Belden Lane noted, "Repeatedly Jesus invites his disciples into the disturbing reality of his grace through inviting them to unanticipated places. . . . Jesus repeatedly leads people into hostile landscapes, away from society and its conventions, to invite them into something altogether new."[3] Jesus was always pushing them beyond their safe, predictable boundaries so they could bring God's love to godforsaken places.

My favorite example of Jesus inviting the disciples to unanticipated places is the story of the Gerasene demoniac. In Mark 5:1, right after they've responded to Jesus' call, we read that Jesus invited them (or dragged them, we're never sure) "across the lake to the region of the Gerasenes." In this place of chaos, brokenness and demonic oppression, they confronted a wild-eyed, untamable and very scary man. This wasn't what the disciples had in mind when Jesus said, "I will make you fishers of men" (Mark 1:17).

Jesus took charge and sent the truckload of demons into a local herd of pigs. Amazingly, the entire herd of two thousand pigs plummeted to their death, and Jesus never apologized. Everyone else was stewing about the pigs (and the loss of income); Jesus focused on one bleeding, marginalized, messy lunatic who was restored to wholeness. At this point, I expect the story to conclude with "And they all praised the power of Jesus" or "They joined Jesus in restoring other broken lives." Instead, we read that they were afraid and "began to plead with Jesus to leave their region" (Mark 5:17).

In effect the crowds say, "Sure, we got this crazy beast of a man who cuts himself with stones and howls through the night and we're all afraid of him, but we've managed to keep it all balanced: the crazy, cutting guy stays in the tomb, we keep our pigs and sell the bacon and chops, and it's all so wrong but it's also safe and predictable. But then Jesus shows up, heals the guy, we lose our money and it's just too weird." As the Misfit, a character in a Flannery O'Connor short story, kept mumbling, "Jesus was the only one to raise the dead, and he shouldn't have done that. He thrown everything off balance."[4] In the story of the pigs and the broken but redeemed man, Jesus did indeed throw everything off balance. So they asked him to leave.

This story is about us and our prayer life. We blithely say, "Prayer changes things"—we even embroider it on pillows—and then we pray nice, decent prayers. We open our lives to Jesus' presence. But then he actually shows up, dragging us into uncomfortable places with strange, broken, marginal people who are out of our social network, and we're tempted to say, "Hey, Jesus, would you mind crawling back into your prayer box? We just can't handle this much Jesus right now."

For example, I pray daily for our four children. So, naturally, when our twenty-year-old son spent a semester in Nairobi, Kenya, I prayed that God would keep him safe. But when Mathew informed me that he was visiting a dangerous slum in the worst part of town, I told him to be careful. When I asked him to take a few pictures, he said, "Oh yeah, about that—they told me not to bring my camera because I'll get robbed and beaten." I quickly prayed harder for his safety, but then I called him and instructed him to avoid the slums. After all my ardent praying and exhorting, Mathew replied, "Dad, I respect you, but I believe that God has called me to serve him in Africa, and if I'm going to be here, I have to see all of it—even the slums. People live here, Dad. Sure, they're poor and desperate and some of them are violent, but I have to do this, Dad." Imagine that: I invoked Jesus, and he "answered" my prayer by calling our son into a dangerous slum. And Jesus called me to the dangerous place of letting my son go. Jesus was asking my son to be a blessing in a godforsaken place, and I had to take the ride.

THE COLLISION OF GOODNESS AND WILDNESS

Of course, talking about prayer as a dangerous activity could make us flee from God if we didn't believe that God is also good. The Bible is clear that God delights in us and in all of his creation (see Genesis

1:31). "'For I know the plans I have for you,' declares the LORD, 'plans to prosper you and not to harm you, plans to give you hope and a future'" (Jeremiah 29:11). Jesus always pointed us to a Father of perfect goodness, a Father who loves to shower his children with good gifts (see Matthew 7:11). And God's good heart is displayed most clearly in the cross, where God was still for us, even in our sin (see Romans 8:31-32). The goodness of God serves as the basis for prayers of supplication (asking God for our needs). Prayer is a relationship with a heavenly Father that involves dialogue, give-and-take, asking and receiving.

But this doesn't imply that Jesus is our "genie-god," a tame and compliant force that constantly bends to our wishes. In the biblical story, God exudes perfect goodness and perfect wildness. Jesus tamed the demoniac, but no one could tame Jesus. They killed Jesus, but they couldn't domesticate him. God's untamable wildness is usually called the freedom of God. God is perfectly free to do as he pleases (see Psalm 135:6), without ceasing to be perfectly good. In other words, in Jesus we find the collision of perfect goodness and perfect wildness.

This past summer I spent a week in a wild place—Libby, Montana, a small town nestled in the Rockies just south of Canada and just east of Idaho. I'm a city boy. Actually it's worse than that: I'm a suburb boy. The suburbs epitomize human safety and control. In the suburbs, everything—maple trees, pet beagles, shrubs, soccer practices, homework and crabgrass—gets carefully planned, controlled and monitored. You rarely spot wild things. But as you drive in the Rockies along the Yaak River, you may suddenly meet a bald eagle, a moose or a grizzly bear. They won't come at your bidding. They'll come when they want to come. You can't control them. You could shoot a grizzly she-bear, but you won't waltz up to her and tame her.

Our problem with prayer is this: we want God to act like a pet beagle, but God is more like a bald eagle. God is free to initiate and define the relationship of covenant love. "You did not choose me, but I chose you" (John 15:16). "I will have mercy on whom I have mercy" (Romans 9:15). "For he chose us in him before the creation of the world" (Ephesians 1:4). Of course, this uncontrollable, untamable, utterly wild God is much more interesting than the genie-god of contemporary fantasies. As the naturalist Doug Peacock once said, "All my life, my favorite animals have been those who could kill and eat me."[5] I love my old, lazy beagle, Dwight, but he doesn't intrigue me as much as a man-eating lion. Wild animals, dangerous animals—like our God—are free and strong and fascinating.

mixing the colors

What happens when you combine these two primary colors—God's goodness and God's wildness—on a theological palette? You get the color of God's jealous love for us. Or we could put it in the following simple theological formula:

God's Perfect Goodness + God's Perfect Wildness =
The Jealous Love of God for Us in Christ

The jealousy of God refers to the way God's goodness and wildness pass through our hearts. God wants to bless our lives with beauty and love (that's his perfect goodness). And God wants our lives to become a blessing to the world around us. But God will bless us and make us a blessing in a way that is consistent with his plans for our lives (God's wildness). As John Webster has written, "[God's jealousy] is his refusal to negotiate away the creature's good by allowing the creature itself to set the terms on which it will live. Certainly, God's jealousy is God's fierce opposition to all that thwarts God's will. . . . But this jealous holiness, precisely in its opposition to and destructiveness of our wickedness, is that which ensures our flourishing."[6]

In other words, God's jealous love consists of his fierce and focused determination to bless us with goodness *on his terms, not ours.* We don't set the terms because God is wild and free. In C. S Lewis's words, in his jealous love God will give us the "full treatment." God's "full treatment" always ensures our flourishing, and it means that God will also bless others through us.

So why is prayer sometimes a dangerous activity? If God is so good, why does he drag us into Gerasene situations so we can meet and greet and even heal deranged demoniacs? Why does he woo or lure us onto boats with unpredictable destinations? Why does God sometimes act like an imbalanced New York cab driver? The short answer is this: because when perfect love and perfect wildness collide, God moves toward us with fierce jealous love. He wants to bless us, but he also wants to bless the world through us. We want prayer to "draw us from a world of care"; God wants prayer to propel us into his world of spiritual growth and service in a world of disintegration and brokenness.

A few months ago a good friend who, by her own admission, isn't a follower of Jesus, invited me to listen to her perform during an open mike night at one of our local bars. So at 10:30 on a Thursday night, I arrived at the Velvet Lounge to hear a few songs by my friend. I was already tired, but I needed to be there for her, and she was delighted that I came to watch her. As I sat at the bar drinking my ice water, I listened to the first act, a lonely young man who read an agonizing (and very long) poem about his unrequited love. The guy on the barstool next to me reached for his beer and said, "S***, I thought he was talking about my love life."

As I listened to another guy croak twelve Led Zeppelin songs, my friend casually leaned over to me and said, "Have I ever told you that I'm really afraid to die? So I'm just not going to die." I said, "You know, you will die some day. It's very certain—like 100 percent." She said, "Well, maybe by the time I reach the age of 103, scientists will be able to attach my head to a young body." I didn't have the heart to tell her that her new brain would make her into another person. My friend kept introducing me as "the pastor down the street." The bartender quipped, "Just so you know, Pastor, I don't trust God anymore." When I asked her to share her story about God, she shrugged it off and told me it would be a long, ugly story.

At midnight my friend finally started her repertoire. I was beat, but I was happy to join her tiny cheering section. I had the suspicion that Jesus might hang out at the Velvet Lounge until midnight to see a friend sing some U2 songs. Nobody howled like the Gerasene demoniac, but this was definitely a place of brokenness and disintegration. This place needed someone to pour out the love of Jesus.

In his jealous love for us, when we invoke Jesus, he will lead us into places of disintegration and brokenness. This doesn't always happen in big and dramatic ways. Sometimes as we open our lives to Jesus, he leads us to share a meal with a lonely family or student, write a letter to someone who is discouraged, forgive someone who has hurt us, step out of our culture and see life through someone else's eyes, volunteer at a homeless shelter, walk with the poor, or care for a small child (perhaps a child with disabilities). These are small, hidden ways that Jesus invites us to go into the world of care by being a blessing to others. As we invoke his name, he will give us "the full treatment," blessing us and sending us to bless the world.

THE SPIRITUAL JOURNEY

When we say that prayer is a dangerous activity, what does that imply for the spiritual journey with Christ? How does that affect how we live before a holy God of jealous love? I'm learning a few life-changing lessons on invoking the name of Jesus.

First, as I pray dangerously, I'm starting to enjoy the glory of God without controlling or at times even comprehending God. God's collision of perfect goodness and perfect wildness sometimes dazzles my mind and soul until I'm reduced to a stunned but joyful silence. The fourth-century theologian Gregory of Nyssa wrote, "When we give a thing a name we imagine we have got hold of it. . . . Perhaps we should do better not to flatter ourselves too soon that we can name God."[7] In other words, just because I can think thoughts about God and make statements for God, it doesn't mean that I have a handle on God. God is larger, better, wilder and more mysterious than I could ever imagine. Even with all my analyzing and explaining, I keep bumping up against the utter incomprehensibility and uncontrollability of our good but free God.

There is a stream in Christian spirituality devoted to this approach to knowing God. According to this stream, sometimes as we pray we learn more about God by what we don't know about God. Throughout the history of the church, this *via negativa* (or negative way) claimed that we must speak about God, and yet all our words about God remain inadequate. God cannot be corralled or grasped with our limited language. "Negative theology" reminds us that when we encounter God's awesome presence, we "find ourselves not simply running short of words but actually speechless and unknowing."[8] At times our best response is to let God dazzle us with his beauty and goodness and majesty.

Last year as I preached some sermons on the nature of the Trinity, I provided definitions, analyses, illustrations, analogies and theological reasoning. All of this was important. We need clear boundaries and concise biblical teaching. But at one point in that sermon series, I suddenly pictured myself as one of those tiny birds that ride on the massive shoulders of a rhinoceros. It would be ludicrous for the bird to assume that it controls the movements of the rhino. Prayer as a dangerous activity was reminding me that I'm not in charge of God either. He's the rhino; I'm the teeny bird.

I'm starting to do that more in my prayer life. Sure, at times I still argue with God and cry out to God, asking clearly for what I need and want. God is my Father, and he invites me to come and ask him for good things. But in my prayer life, I'm also starting to feel more like the teeny bird. And like the teeny bird, I realize that I don't ever corral the rhino; I climb on and enjoy the ride.

As we pray dangerously we can enjoy the adventure of serving Christ in unanticipated places. Jesus the boundary pusher brings us to dangerous places. Again, this makes life a grand adventure. I love the scene in *The Hobbit* when Gandalf appears at Bilbo's front door and says, "I am looking for someone to share in an adventure I am arranging, and it's very difficult to find anyone."

Bilbo replies, "I should think so—in these parts! We are plain quiet folk and have no use for adventures. Nasty disturbing uncomfortable things! Make you late for dinner! I can't think what anybody sees in them."

And then Bilbo waited for Gandalf to go away. But the old man didn't move, making Bilbo "a little cross." Finally Bilbo said, "We don't want any adventures here, thank you! You might try over The Hill or across The Water."[9]

But as we know, Bilbo, like Abraham and Jesus' disciples, went on the adventure. His whole life became an adventure. We often treat Jesus like Bilbo treated Gandalf. After Jesus healed the demoniac in Mark 5, everyone pleaded with him to go away. Then in the very next chapter, Jesus returned to his hometown, and his own people "took offense at him" (Mark 6:3). The Greek word for "offense" is the word *skandalon,* from which we get the English word *scandal.* They were scandalized by Jesus—put off, repelled, made uncomfortable. And then the story concludes by saying, "He could not do any miracles there, except lay his hands on a few sick people and heal them" (Mark 6:5).

Apparently we only have two options in our prayer lives:

1. We can become scandalized by Jesus, resent his presence and his constant interruptions, insist that Jesus stop sending us into places of brokenness and pain, and demand that prayer be "sweet"; or
2. we can invoke his presence and then joyfully adjust our lives according to his interruptions.

If we choose the second option, Jesus will lead us into unlikely places with unlikely people for an uncommonly interesting (and sometimes uncomfortable) life. We can resent the intrusion or enjoy the adventure of a lifetime.

I'm starting to enjoy the adventure.

9

PRAYER AS PAYING ATTENTION

I've struggled my whole life to pay attention. My second-grade teacher, Miss Drill (yes, that was her real name), first diagnosed my problem of inattentiveness. Then in ninth grade, my high school basketball coach, Mr. Hammerstein (yes, that was his real name), also noticed my lack of focus. Mr. Hammerstein (or "The Hammer," as we called him behind his back), was a gigantic man with hands like grizzly paws. He was a soft-spoken gentle man, but on one occasion he erupted with what I still call "The Hammer Speech." During halftime, after I had played the most uninspired basketball of my brief career, as "The Hammer" lectured wildly about basketball fundamentals, I had one of my finer ADD moments: I stared out the locker room door and burst into a massive yawn. "The Hammer" grabbed me by the jersey, lifted me off the bench and screamed in my face, "Woodley, if I don't see you focus in the second half, I will pour gasoline down your shorts, light you on fire and we'll all watch you run around and burn. You got that, son?" Needless to say, I played that second half with unrelenting intensity.

It's little wonder that later in life I was diagnosed with "Attention Deficit Disorder—Inattentive Type." Apparently ADD doesn't have anything to do with your IQ (that's what they tell me, anyway). But people with ADD also must learn new, lifelong strategies and techniques for focusing and paying attention. In a strange way, studying ADD has given me a fresh perspective on my prayer life. I'm convinced that one of the main reasons we don't pray is simply this: we're inattentive to God; our soul under-functions, and we lose our focus.

Jesus certainly knew about the struggle with spiritual attentiveness. Throughout his life, Jesus kept saying things like "Stay alert," "Keep watch" and "Don't fall asleep." As he approached his death, these reminders grew in frequency and intensity (see Mark 13:5, 34, 35, 37; 14:11, 34, 37, 38). At one point Jesus compared the time of his coming to the days of Noah, when "people were eating and drinking, marrying and giving in marriage" (Matthew 24:38). Obviously Jesus wasn't anti-eating or anti-marriage; the problem was much deeper. When the flood finally came, no one saw it coming because they forgot to focus. So Jesus drove the point home by saying, "Therefore keep watch" (Matthew 24:42).

Jesus continued by comparing himself to a burglar who comes "at an hour when you do not expect him" (Matthew 24:44). Like a burglar, Jesus will break in and disrupt your life. Like a burglar, Jesus is sneaky and subtle. But unlike a burglar, you really want to meet this break-in artist. So watch out and stay on full alert when he starts sneaking into your life.

For Jesus, prayer begins with attentiveness: stay awake, keep watch, don't fall asleep. So naturally, Christian writers have noticed the connection between attentiveness and our prayer life. Emilie Griffin said simply that "the essence of prayer is to give God our full attention."[1] Thomas Merton claimed that we're all like pilots of fog-bound steamers, "peering into the gloom in front of us, listening for the sounds of other ships, and we can only reach our harbor if we keep alert. The spiritual life is, then, first of all a matter of keeping awake."[2]

NOW FOR SOME BAD NEWS

Here's the bad news about paying attention to God: it's hard! I could start by blaming external factors. Even at the end of the nineteenth century, Friedrich Nietzsche claimed that "the massive influx of impressions is so great; surprising, barbaric, and violent things press so overpoweringly—'balled up in hideous clumps'—in the youthful soul; that it can save itself only by taking recourse in premeditated stupidity." In other words, every day we're bombarded with numerous "impressions" (i.e., advertisements, demands, noise, gadgets) that press on us so "overpoweringly" that we can escape only by becoming "stupid." For Nietzsche, "stupidity" didn't refer to a diminished IQ but a numbed inattentiveness. As a contemporary critic noted, "People at the end of the nineteenth century were suffocating in a vast goo of meaningless stimulation."[3]

That was a hundred years ago. I'd argue that the "vast goo of meaningless stimulation" has grown deeper, thicker, vaster and, well, gooier. A recent *New York Times* article, titled "Product Packages Now Shout to Get Your Attention," noted that advertisers are vying to grab our shriveled attention spans. Over the past hundred years, Pepsi had changed the look of its bottles or cans only ten times. Now they switch designs every few weeks. Kleenex stuck with its square or rectangular boxes for forty years before adding oval boxes. In the 1990s most companies retained their packaging designs for seven years or more. Now they are changing their package designs an average of every two years. According to one marketing expert, "We can't get [people] to sit down and listen to our argument."[4] Marketers have to keep grabbing our ever-shrinking attention spans.

Unfortunately, my spiritual inattentiveness also resides *inside* my heart. Most of us have the same problem, so try this experiment: for a whole day shut off everything—the television, iPod, radio, cell phone, e-mail and your mouth. If you're anything like me, this experiment will make you very antsy. When the poet Denise Levertov tried to pray, she lamented, "I stop to think about you, and my mind at once like a minnow darts away into the shadows. . . . Not for one second will my self hold still, but wanders anywhere, everywhere it can turn."[5] It's offensive but accurate: I have the spiritual attention span of a minnow.

THE GOOD NEWS ABOUT OUR INATTENTION

Fortunately, the Bible offers hope for spiritually inattentive people: God cares about my spiritual attention deficit problem, and he wants to help me. According to the Bible, God *has* to help me or I'll keep acting like Levertov's minnow, darting here and there like a frantic, small-minded slippery creature without ever resting in God. We could call this the *really* bad news about our inattentiveness. At one point Jesus reached back in the history of his people and quoted the prophet Isaiah: "You will be ever hearing but never understanding; you will be ever seeing but never perceiving. For this people's heart has become calloused; they hardly hear with their ears, and they have closed their eyes" (Matthew 13:14-15; see also Isaiah 6:9-10). All throughout the Old Testament, God kept calling out to his people, saying, "Listen, listen, listen!" But just like us, they had an inbuilt problem: "they did not listen or pay attention; instead, they followed the stubbornness of their evil hearts" (Jeremiah 11:8).

Surprisingly, this is good news. First of all, it places everyone on a level playing field. We all have a fundamental problem: spiritually speaking, we're about as attentive as a corpse. There aren't two classes of human beings: the spiritually enlightened, attentive types, and the spiritual dolts who constantly lose focus. Second, this *really* bad news about spiritual attentiveness invites us into a truly gospel-centered spiritual life. Paying attention in our prayer life doesn't start with practicing a few spiritual disciplines or screwing up our faces (or our souls) with extra concentration. It starts with a supernatural spiritual operation. That's why the Bible refers to following Jesus with radical terms like having a "new birth" and being "born again." We can't do it ourselves; God does it in us and for us as we trust in Jesus Christ. Faith is never our gift to God; faith is God's gift to us.

Once we receive this gift of salvation, we don't pray to make God accept us; we pray because God has already accepted us. The entire Trinity gets involved in this radical operation. God the Father raises us from spiritual death. Our role is to trust, remaining dependent on and open to the power of the Holy Spirit. Jesus, the One who commands us to "Stay awake!" is the same one who lives within us to empower our attentiveness.

THE GREATEST AWAKENER

God awakens us and rebirths us in his power and from his own initiative. From start to finish, it's a process and a reality called grace. God does it for us even when we don't deserve it and even when we aren't looking for it. I like to put it this way: according to the Bible, we're all on an exciting spiritual journey—away from God. Some people are surprised by this kind of language, but I know that I've never truly sought after God on my own initiative. Left to myself, I never liked God and I certainly didn't want to "find" him. "Spirituality" never bothered me, nor did "world religions," "the supernatural" or even "the occult." I just dreaded meeting Jesus in a dark alley somewhere. I never thought he'd beat me up; I just thought he'd turn me into a miserable freak.

For most of my growing-up years, Jesus was like my younger brother. He used to tag along, but we never let him play with us. He just kept asking, "Can I play with you?" Jesus seemed to say the same thing, and then I'd tell Jesus the same thing we always told my brother: "Watch the lips: GO AWAY! Leave us alone!" But Jesus didn't go away. He didn't budge. He just stood there like a huge, fierce, sad-eyed lion. Jesus, the menacing, teary-eyed stalker of my heart.

But somehow Jesus broke through to me. I often say that "I accepted Jesus as my Lord and Savior," but that's only the last part of the story. The real story is that he just kept hanging around, pursuing me like a patient but very hungry lion until he finally pounced on me and tore my chest wide open with his love. I talk like I chose him (and in one sense I did choose him), but more than anything, he chose me, even when I was fleeing his presence. I was dirty, lost, confused, hungry and defiant; but he kept chasing me until he found me, embraced me and brought me back home. That's the gospel. That's grace.

Grace is the great awakening for slumbering, inattentive souls. I need grace reminders every day or at least every week if possible. A few weeks ago my friend Jim gave me a grace awakening by inviting me to hand out food in an abandoned parking lot on the edge of our posh Long Island community. After hearing a short sermon, a group of about thirty hungry and ragged men and women lined up to receive dented canned goods, day-old bread, zucchini, eggplants and cartons of soy milk. It sure wasn't a banquet, but they were eager and open. So they came—Caucasian, black and Latino; babies and senior citizens; married and single; addicts and the unemployed.

As they lined up to receive the food, God gave me a vision: I was in church, my church, as we lined up for the Lord's Supper. Most of us came with nice, clean clothes. None of us smelled of body odor or cheap wine. All of us drove expensive cars as we came from fine houses with intact families. Our children play travel soccer and plan to attend college, an Ivy League school if possible. But in my vision I saw that the parking lot line and the nice church line were exactly the same line. God doesn't see two lines. Both lines contain men and women hungry for food, for love and for God's grace.

Grace is the single most powerful awakener in our spiritual lives. Fear, guilt, pain, suffering, failure—they all have their place in God's plan to help us stay alert, but nothing works like grace. Grace is God's first and best "technique" to wake up our drowsy souls. In other words, when we slip into spiritual inattentiveness, God's first speech is something like, "Behold, what manner of love the Father has given to us that we should be called the sons of God" (see 1 John 3:1; this is the way I remembered the verse). In other words, God says, "Look, behold, remember and wake up when you see and feel and know once again how much I love you!"

LESSONS FROM AN UNEXPECTED FRIEND

I sincerely wish that recalling God's grace would be sufficient to keep me awake. If God let me design my spiritual journey, I'd prefer this simple process for staying spiritually alert: come every week for a sermon, some worship songs and the Lord's Supper until grace sinks into the brain, and then we can go home. But so far God hasn't asked for my advice. Against my will and against my suggestion, he has included another very crucial element in arousing my spiritual alertness: pain. On most occasions, pain isn't the enemy of spiritual attentiveness; it's a better friend than pleasure or success.

Unfortunately, I've had a very shallow, glib understanding of pain. I've often quoted C. S. Lewis's famous line about pain to suffering people: "God whispers to us in our pleasures, speaks in our conscience, but shouts in our pain: it is His megaphone to rouse a deaf world."[6] I throw it out there like I'm tossing someone a soft, fuzzy peach: "Here you go, good fellow, take a bite of this juicy peach." In my insensitivity, I didn't know that I was actually throwing people a live hand grenade.

In the past few years here's the first lesson I've learned about pain: it hurts! Apparently I was a newbie at pain. I've spent most of my life moving upward in a fairly pain-free existence, but in the past few years I've encountered significant pain. You don't need my details because you probably have your own story of pain. You know how much life can hurt. I also know from personal experience that when I try to avoid or numb the pain, it will eventually get even worse.

Here's the second key lesson about pain: it works! God uses it to get my attention. I don't like this concept. I prefer a nice God who will take my pain away and cast it into the deepest sea (thankfully God does that with my sin, but he doesn't do it with my pain). I want God to make me successful and comfortable. But in one way or another, Jesus has told us that a blessed life isn't a pain-free life. "Blessed are the poor in spirit. . . . Blessed are those who mourn. . . . Blessed are those who hunger and thirst. . . . Blessed are those who are persecuted" (Matthew 5:3-10). He constantly referred to his own path of pain: "The Son of Man will be betrayed. . . . They will condemn him to death . . . to be mocked and flogged and crucified" (Matthew 20:18-19).

For Jesus, the gentle stream of God's blessing carries us right into the land of suffering. Why does he arrange the spiritual life this way? Why does he lead us on a path that includes pain? Honestly, I don't always know, and pain can come from many sources. But I do know this: God has used it to get my attention. I can't ignore pain. And I also know that my heart isn't just distracted; it can also grow arrogant, calloused, shallow and addicted to lesser gods. Sometimes the best thing God can do—and perhaps it's the only thing for God—is to grant me the gift of pain.

The Franciscan priest Richard Rohr was speaking about male spirituality when he said, "Once we reach the age of thirty, success has nothing to teach us. Success is fun and rewarding, but we don't learn anything new from it. It's not a bad friend; it's just a lousy teacher. The only thing that can teach us, that can get through to us and profoundly change us, is suffering, failure, loss and wounds."[7] Rohr said the same thing in his book *Adam's Return:* "All great spirituality is about what we do with our pain. . . . It seems that nothing less than some kind of pain will force us to release our grip on our small expectations and our self-serving illusions."[8]

Once again, I resent this, but Jesus and the rest of the Bible concur: pain hurts, but in terms of getting our attention, it also works. Pain often functions as God's "Hammer Speech." The psalmist said it so succinctly: "Before I was afflicted I went astray, but now I obey your word" (Psalm 119:67). Through pain, God gives a harsh but gracious wake-up call to distracted, lethargic creatures who are content to coast miserably on the spiritual path.

OUR PART IN WAKING UP

Perhaps I've made it sound like God does everything for us. I keep falling asleep on God, but he keeps tapping me on the shoulder and whispering, "Hey—it's time to wake up." But I certainly have my part to play in staying alert to God. It requires effort to stay focused and attentive. My friend Ray from my first church in northeastern Minnesota kept telling me, "Just give me the 'KISS' course to God—'Keep It Simple, Stupid'—because I'm pretty lazy, busy and I'm in a hurry." Aren't we all? That's why staying alert involves relinquishing our lazy, harried demands for instant, effort-free spiritual success.

The brilliant twentieth-century French thinker Simone Weil defined attention as a "just and loving concentration upon some individual or situation."[9] In this sense, paying attention requires the same type of effort that's needed for navigating other areas of life. Weil used school studies as a low-level example of paying attention. It doesn't matter whether you're studying geometry or Spanish or statistics; what matters is that you learn to pay attention, to keep focused and to concentrate on a certain subject, "ready to receive in its naked truth the object that is to penetrate it."

So in one sense we practice attentiveness all the time. When I was in sixth grade, my parents bought me a small microscope out of the JCPenney Christmas catalog. I immediately went to the local pond, drilled a hole in the ice and started paying attention to the living things under the surface. If you were to sit beside me while I'm watching our fourteen-year-old son play soccer, I probably wouldn't speak to you. I can't multitask at a soccer game because I'm attending to my son. When you're watching a good movie, reading clear prose, making soup, changing a tire or watching football, you are paying attention. And according to Weil, "Without our knowing or feeling it, this apparently barren effort has brought more light into the soul. The result will one day be discovered in prayer."

In terms of our busy, distracted, hyperspeed culture, how do we obey Jesus' simple command to "keep watch"? What is our part in focusing on not just a random subject but the subject of God, who is also the Ultimate Object and Subject and who makes tiny subjects out of all of us?

SAVORING THE CHOCOLATE CAKE: THE POWER OF MEDITATION

The primary spiritual discipline I've discovered for increasing our attentiveness to God is the discipline of meditation. In the biblical tradition, meditation doesn't imply an emptying of the mind. It begins with clear thinking and reasoning. Meditation can build off of our study, but it also involves much more than reasoning. Study involves reading and thinking so we can know the truth about a subject or topic. When we meditate, we try to absorb and identify with what we've already taken in. So when the early Christians meditated on the Psalms, they didn't just analyze them; they savored them, repeating the words slowly, thoughtfully, allowing the words of Scripture to descend from the mind into the heart.

Study versus meditation: it's the difference between analyzing a recipe for double-chocolate cake and eating the cake, allowing the rich, dark chocolate to melt in your mouth, savoring every rich and delicious bite. You do need to study the recipe. Then you need to purchase and organize all the ingredients. But eventually you'll want to make it and eat it so you can savor it. Savoring is the point of a chocolate cake. Meditation leads us to the point of savoring God's Word.

In other words, meditation always leads to love, intimacy and delight.[10] Danish philosopher Søren Kierkegaard said that someone meditating on the Bible should resemble a lover who has just received a long letter from his beloved. When the lover opens the letter, he doesn't grab a dictionary, dissecting the text and defining all the words. No, he reads it like a lover. Attending to God's Word with a detached, unloving heart can lead us further from God's truth. That's why Kierkegaard bristled with disdain when people merely analyzed God's Word:

> Being alone with God's word is a dangerous matter. Of course, you can always find ways to defend yourself against it: Take the Bible, lock your door—but then get out ten dictionaries and twenty-five commentaries. Then you can read it just as calmly and coolly as you read newspaper advertising. . . . Can't we be honest for once! We have become such experts at cunningly shoving one layer after another, one interpretation after another, between the Word and our lives, (much in the way a boy puts a napkin or more under his pants when he is going to get a licking), and we then allow this preoccupation to swell to such profundity that we never come to look at ourselves in the mirror.

> Yes, it seems as if all this research and pondering and scrutinizing would draw God's Word very close to us. Yet this interpreting and re-interpreting and scholarly research and new scholarly research is but a defense against it.[11]

Instead, according to Kierkegaard, a lover will read a love letter slowly, carefully, attentively. His eyes will sparkle with delight. He will say the words out loud. The lover will commit his beloved's words to memory. He will lay the letter down only to pick it up and read it again. He will savor the letter like we'd savor rich, dark chocolate.

What does this love-based meditation look like? Take a simple passage like Psalm 42:1-2: "As the deer pants for streams of water, so my soul pants for you, O God. My soul thirsts for God, for the living God." I could study it by exploring the psalm's historical background as exilic poetry, duly noting the parallelism of Hebrew poetry, astutely observing that the words "pant" and "thirst" compliment each other. Yes, indeed, most interesting! Study does have a place, but as an end in itself, it may take me further from God's presence.

But when I meditate, I read the words slowly and carefully. I repeat them over and over again, perhaps memorizing and recalling them during the day. As the words move from my lips and my brain into the depths of my heart, I start to identify with them. It's not just interesting; now *I'm* the deer panting for streams. *I'm* panting for God. I feel the thirst within me. And according to Psalm 42:8 ("By day the LORD directs his love"), I begin to savor God's love for me in the midst of my thirsting. That is meditation.

LOVING THE QUESTIONS: THE POWER OF PONDERING

As we meditate on God's Word, we also start to listen to the themes of our own life as well. I prefer the word *pondering* for this stage of our spiritual attentiveness. Pondering is stereophonic listening: it's the place where I listen to God's Word and my life. How is God's Word intersecting in my life? Am I meditating on a portion of God's Word that is actually coming to life right now? How is Jesus leading me to follow him through these circumstances?

Mary is my brightest mentor in the tradition of pondering prayer. After the birth of Jesus, we're told that she "treasured up all these things and *pondered* them in her heart" (Luke 2:19). In other words, she was listening to God's Word and to her own life. At this point in the Gospel story, the events are overwhelming and confusing. The Savior of the world has been born in a stable, and she is the mother of our Lord. Angelic choruses and shepherds have come to adore the child. Soon an old man named Simeon will bless Jesus and tell Mary, "A sword will pierce your own soul too" (Luke 2:35).

From Mary's example I noticed the essential nature of pondering prayer. Pondering prayer begins with meditation on God's Word and God's activity. What is God saying? What are the themes of God's good work in the world? I stay with God's Word and pay attention to God's revelation. But as I meditate I also start to ask, "Where is God's Word intersecting with my life?" So as I pay attention to God's Word, I'm also paying attention to God's good work in my life. I listen with both ears of my heart.

Mary was surrounded by marvelous, world-changing events. God was working and revealing the beauty of his redemptive love for the world. But God was also at work in her life. What does it all mean? How is God speaking to and through Mary's life? As Mary treasures these things in her heart and she ponders them all, God doesn't give her quick answers or easy resolutions. Instead, she learns to live with the questions, dwelling in God's presence, making connections between her life and God's grand plan, remaining open and alert and attentive before God. God is certainly up to something beautiful, and Mary wants to stay awake for it.

Pondering welcomes questions and tension. When Mary pondered, God didn't grant an immediate resolution to her tension. Actually the Gospel story hints that the questions probably grew even more intense. Did she understand Jesus' dangerous, controversial ministry and his shocking claims about himself? Did she resolve the dilemma and pain of the cross, watching her son die naked and alone? Mary probably pondered again and again without getting quick answers to her questions.

When we ponder, we learn to love what poet Franz Wright calls "the long silences" of life.[12] The answers to our questions, the resolution to our tension, will come someday, but we trust God to unfurl the answers in his timing.

Pondering prayer also trusts the unseen, overarching and utterly good purposes of God. God is writing something beautiful into our lives and into the world, but we don't have the whole script. When we ponder, we dare to ask and even love our questions because God is good even when we don't have the answers. In the United Methodist hymnal, there's a prayer in the liturgy for evening prayer that praises God because "all day long you are stirring us up for good in this world." Pondering assumes that God is at work. God is stirring us up for good in this world. I can trust that even when I can't see the end of the process.

Pondering doesn't follow a formula, but let me share my portrait of pondering. About two years ago one of my sons asked me to read through the entire Bible and jot down my personal commentary. During this three-year project (and at times it was a project), I started to notice over and over again the Bible's clear teaching about caring for the poor. It even hit me in Leviticus, but it struck me again and again in the long section of the prophets. I started meditating on passages like Isaiah 58, which says, "If you do away with the yoke of oppression . . . if you spend yourselves in behalf of the hungry and satisfy the needs of the oppressed, then your light will rise in the darkness, and your night will become like the noonday" (Isaiah 58:9-10). Every week I'd read something similar. Obviously, God was trying to teach me something, so I started to pay attention to his Word.

Meanwhile, I could also see the circumstances of my life intersecting with this biblical meditation. By "chance," while I was waiting for a delayed flight in Midway Airport, I picked up a strange magazine, turned to the back editorial and read an article on world poverty. The article moved me to tears, stirring a deep reservoir of compassion buried in my heart.[13] By "chance" I started looking through an old photo album that contained pictures from our trip to the Pringle Home Orphanage in the Blue Mountains of Jamaica. All the sights, sounds, smells and even tastes from more than twenty years ago started flooding back into my memory. Then by "chance" our twenty-year-old son went to Africa and told me about his weekly ventures into the wretched slums of Nairobi, Kenya. When he told me he had to do this (even against my objections), it shook me to the core.

God was awakening my heart not with answers (because I had no idea what to do with all these circumstances) but with disturbing questions. But the Word of God and the reality of my life were intersecting. So I started to ponder the following questions: Why do I live in one of the richest countries in the world? As a follower of Jesus, what is my responsibility to the poorest of the poor? After a few years of meditating on the Bible and pondering my life's circumstances, God finally led me to connect with Saul Cruz in Mexico City and his Armonia Ministries. But notice the pattern: the questions lead to tension, the tension compels us to ponder our prayers before God, and then we are led to action.

Pondering prayer happens all the time. We ponder through our life as we look back on each day and ask the following questions:

> What portions of God's Word struck my heart? For instance, perhaps I read about God's forgiveness, and my heart is stirred. Do I know why? What does this say about my life? Is there some unresolved guilt lodged in my heart? As we ponder, we ask and pay attention to God's Word and our questions about God's Word.
>
> What positive signs of the Holy Spirit's work in my life did I see today?
>
> Where did I fail God or others yesterday? What can I learn from those experiences? (Remember: only a gracious and patient God would show you your sins without judging you on the spot.)
>
> What are the themes of God's good work in my life? This question grows out of a regular pondering of my life before God's presence. As I listen, as I ponder before God, the themes will start to emerge.[14]

I'm learning to attend to these questions. They seldom get resolved quickly. There's often tension. They need time and space to grow quietly within me, but like Mary, I'm learning to ponder well.

THE FRUIT OF PAYING ATTENTION TO GOD

What happens as we grow in attentiveness? How does God shape our souls and our love as we learn to stay alert? What is the fruit of spiritual attentiveness?

As we grow in attentiveness, we'll start to notice God's good work in us in the ordinary places of life. We realize that God may be speaking to us often, but we just aren't listening. Now as we pray with an attentive heart and mind, the presence, power and love of God appear in surprising places and times. For instance, during a recent dark time in my life, I felt an overwhelming sense of insecurity and confusion. I was asking God (and asking my friends to ask God) for resolution. I told my friend Ron, a wise Christian counselor, "I just need more security in my life." Ron rudely interrupted with three words: "Security is overrated." At the time, I resented Ron's comment. *That's it?* I thought. *That's your best shot at helping me—"security is overrated"?* But for some reason the words lodged deep within my chest.

Ron didn't quote the Bible, but his words certainly resonated with biblical themes. In that sense, they were living and active and sharper than any two-edged sword (Hebrews 4:12). Oh, they cut deep and clean. Ron was right: I was inflating the value of and the demand for security in this life. After all, did God say, "Walk by your own security" or "Walk by faith"? I knew the answer. I'm learning to pay attention to the presence of a loving, powerful God even in the midst of circumstances that feel incredibly insecure. When we're attentive, we start to notice God's activity anywhere and anytime.

My heart and my mind still wander away from God. I'm distracted and inattentive. I'm still like that darting, slippery minnow. But I realize more than ever how much God longs to speak to me, to grab my attention and help me pay attention. He wants it more than I do. Sometimes it comes in the sweetness of a "Look how much I love you." Sometimes God speaks through the pain of a "Hammer Speech." Sometimes I have to apply the discipline of meditating on his Word and pondering how it intersects with my life. But he always brings me back to his great grace. As the old hymn says,

> Prone to wander, Lord, I feel it;
> prone to leave the God of love.
> Here's my heart, O take and seal it,
> seal it for Thy courts above.

10

PRAYER AS FEELING GOD'S HEARTBEAT

According to a Jewish story, once upon a time there was a four-year-old boy named Mortakai who refused to attend school and study Hebrew. Whenever his parents tried to immerse his mind in the Torah, he would sneak away and play on the swing set. Every form of persuasion failed. Mortakai remained stubborn and defiant. The exasperated parents even brought him to a famous psychiatrist, but that also proved futile. Nothing changed the young boy's heart, which seemed to grow more distant, lonely and hardened every week.

Finally, in utter desperation, Mortakai's parents brought him to the local rabbi, a warm and wise spiritual guide. As the parents explained their plight, pouring out their frustration and despair, the rabbi listened intently. Without saying a word, he gently picked up Mortakai, took him in his arms and held him close to his chest. The rabbi held Mortakai close enough and tight enough so the young boy could feel the safe, rhythmic beating of the rabbi's heart. Then, still without a word, he gently handed the child back to his parents. From that point on, Mortakai listened to his parents, studied the Torah and only occasionally slipped away to play on the swing set.[1]

Sometimes prayer means listening to God's heartbeat. When we're sad or lonely or we just keep wandering away from God, we need God our Father to pick us up and hold us close to his chest so we can hear his heartbeat. In other words, we need to come and remain in God's presence with one agenda: to be with God, resting, lingering, delighting in God's love. In the history of Christian spirituality, "prayer as feeling God's heartbeat" goes by the name "contemplative prayer." I've placed contemplative prayer near the end of this book because, though it's an old and deep and rich prayer path, in our culture it's largely misunderstood and certainly underpracticed.

THE WOMAN WHO HEARD JESUS' HEARTBEAT (AND THE ONE WHO DIDN'T)

Throughout the ages Christian thinkers and spiritual guides have offered diverse definitions for contemplative prayer. It is "an intimate sharing between friends . . . taking time to frequently be alone with [God] who we know loves us."[2] It's not "so much a way to find God as a way of resting in him . . . who loves us."[3] It's like falling in love (with God) on a starlit Syrian night.[4] It's the "knowledge of God that is impregnated with love."[5] It begins when we release our obsession of doing things for God and others so we can say, "I am in God's presence, what a joy, let us be still."[6]

These definitions flow from a key biblical theme: those who trust in Jesus can draw near to God the Father (see Hebrews 7:18-19). Through Jesus our great high priest, the One who has abolished our sin (see Colossians 2:13-15), we can even cry out with childlike faith, "*Abba*, Father" (Romans 8:15, emphasis in original). This is a picture of intimacy with a Father who loves us, a Savior who embraces us and a Spirit who pours love into us. This triune God invites us to come into his presence with childlike trust. There are times in this new relationship when we won't ask for anything. We won't argue or groan or take a dangerous journey; we'll just sit with God and listen to the safe, rhythmic beating of his heart. And like Mortakai, hearing and feeling God's heart will heal our broken lives.

The classic definitions listed above also find their roots in a tiny, delightful Gospel story about living and praying as a true contemplative, and how to live as an anti-contemplative (see Luke 10:38-42). Notice that this tiny story appears right after Jesus' famous story about a good Samaritan (see Luke 10:25-37). In that story a band of thugs beat a traveler and left him bleeding by the side of the road. Everyone carefully avoided the bleeding body until a racially despised Samaritan man displayed costly, time-consuming mercy to the beaten man. Then Jesus told us that we should "go and do likewise" (Luke 10:37). Clearly Jesus wants us to respond to human needs with an active display of God's mercy. But as we'll see in the next story, Jesus' intent is for our doing-for-others life to flow from our being-with-Jesus life.

So Luke 10:38 begins by describing the next scene: "As Jesus and his disciples were on their way, he came to a village where a woman named Martha opened her home to him." When Martha "opened her home to him," she got Jesus, but she also got his entire motley gang of smelly, sweaty, hungry and grumpy disciples. But Martha, the efficient hostess, the maestro of hospitality, the get-it-done woman of excellence, started preparing a feast for the small mob. While she was actually doing something, living as a good Samaritan in her own home, we find Mary acting lazy and unproductive, refusing to meet the human needs around her. For all practical purposes, Mary was merely wasting her time by sitting "at the Lord's feet listening to what he said" (Luke 10:39).

As Mary felt the heartbeat of Jesus, Martha churned with internal strife. In Luke 10:40 we read that she "was distracted by all the preparations [literally, 'much serving'] that had to be made." The urgent tasks on her to-do list yanked her in seventeen different directions. Finally, as her frustration mounted, she snapped at Jesus: "Lord, don't you care that my sister has left me to do the work by myself?" And then she barked out an order: "Tell her to help me!"

Even though she's frustrated, angry, demanding and controlling, I tend to side with Martha. She's doing all the work. She's productive and efficient, and Mary isn't helping at all. So Jesus *should* say, "Hey, everyone, Martha's right. Mary, get off your duff and start helping your sister. We have a busy schedule here—eating, preaching, praying, healing the sick, saving the lost, liberating the oppressed, changing the world—so let's get productive like Martha and see some servanthood in action!" Instead, Jesus gently rebukes Martha by replying, "Martha, Martha, . . . you are worried and upset about many things, but only one thing is needed. Mary has chosen what is better, and it will not be taken away from her" (Luke 10:41-42).

What is the "one thing" that Mary has chosen, the "one thing" that is better and that will not be taken away from her? Literally, the "one thing" refers to Mary's posture and practice of being with Jesus and listening intently to the rhythm of his heart. In traditional language of prayer, Mary is praying and living contemplatively.

I Tried It . . . I Didn't Like It

Fifteen years ago I experimented with an extended period of contemplative prayer. It all started with an article in the *Minneapolis Star & Tribune*. At the time, we were living in a small town (460 people, to be precise) in northeastern Minnesota. Fresh out of seminary, brimming with big plans to change the world for Jesus and turn "my" teeny church into "Willow Creek of the Northland," I eventually started to burn out. My soul was famished, and I had no idea how to feed it. That's when I spotted the front-page article on contemplative prayer. Apparently the author had visited Pacem in Terris, a retreat center in central Minnesota, merely as a curious journalist. He liked it so much that he spent a week in one of their hermitages, a small cabin situated on 220 acres of prairie grass, birch trees and swampland.

I don't know if "God spoke to me" through the article; I just knew that the article awakened a deep hunger within me to know God better. So I "tried" contemplative prayer. When I arrived at Pacem in Terris, they handed me a basket of homemade bread, a hunk of cheddar cheese, a gigantic bran muffin stuffed with nuts and dates, and a gallon jug filled with spring water. Then I trekked deep into the prairie grass to find my hermitage as the Pacem staff promised to pray for my journey to "be still with God." Wow, for the next twenty-four hours I would finally live as a real contemplative!

It was awful. I felt lazy, useless and unproductive. I was wasting my time, and more importantly I was wasting God's precious time. I wasn't doing anything to change the world for Jesus' sake. I just kept falling asleep on God. Honestly, I just couldn't help it, so I spent about 75 percent of my time on the bed, slipping into a semicomatose state. Although I enjoyed the basket of food (and kept wandering back to the Pacem office to sneak another bran muffin), I didn't enjoy "being still with God." Instead, I kept thinking, *And what's the point of this? What am I supposed to get out of this? How is this supposed to feed me and help change the world for Jesus' sake? Am I really doing God a favor by snoozing in the woods?*

Throughout the past fifteen years I've met others who feel the same way about contemplative prayer. They don't object to the concept. To the contrary, after years of "deep" and "meaty" Bible teaching, wordy worship services and frantically paced church calendars, they hunger to listen to God's heartbeat. Sadly, they almost never arrive at the point of saying, "I am in God's presence; what a joy! Let us be still." Sitting at Jesus' feet seems intriguing, but it also sounds as impractical as lounging on the beaches of Tahiti for a few weeks. With so much important stuff to get done, who has time to sit in God's lap or wallow in white sands by the Pacific Ocean?

After my abysmal belly flop into contemplative prayer, I can still relate to these sentiments. But I also can't ignore Jesus' straightforward claim that Mary's practice remains the "one thing" necessary for our spiritual lives. In other words, Jesus stressed that our active life *for God* must continually flow from our inner life *with God*. In Jesus' mind, this wasn't optional. He wasn't suggesting two paths—the Martha path or the Mary path—and then allowing us to choose. In our culture 98 percent of us would choose the Martha path. For Jesus there's only one path: the Mary path.

This doesn't mean that we withdraw entirely from the world, cease all activity and just contemplate. But it does mean that we can't follow

Jesus and serve him in the world without regularly drawing close and listening to our Father's heartbeat. The apostle Paul provided the best summary of Christian spirituality when he said, "I have been crucified with Christ and I no longer live, but Christ lives in me. The life I live in the body, I live by faith in the Son of God, who loved me and gave himself for me" (Galatians 2:20). Contemplative prayer means centering our lives on the "one thing" reality that *"Christ lives in me."* We pray, rest in, feed on and enjoy God until those four words—*Christ lives in me*—become larger, better, tastier, richer, deeper than anything else in our lives.

SIPPING GRAPE JUICE WITH CLYDE

Praying and living contemplatively continued to feel abstract, unnecessary and maybe even wasteful until I started sipping grape juice with Clyde. Visiting Clyde provided a handle for me to understand contemplative prayer. Clyde was a ninety-one-year-old Norwegian widower from my teeny church in northeastern Minnesota. Before I arrived in town, Clyde had spent ten years caring for his wife as she slipped into the darkness of Alzheimer's. Every day for ten years (he never missed), Clyde visited Eileen and spoon-fed her breakfast and lunch. After her death, Clyde moved to the local senior citizen's home. By the time I met him, he was nearly deaf. So week after week, as we sat in dual rocking chairs, I would yell my way through our typical conversation:

"HOW ARE YOU DOING TODAY, CLYDE?'

"Oh, not bad." ("Not bad" in Minnesotan means "pretty darn good.")

Short silence.

"NICE WEATHER OUT THERE, EH?"

"What did you say?"

"NICE WEATHER OUT THERE."

"Oh, yeah, sure, you betcha. We could use some rain, but not bad."

Longer silence.

"SO, ARE YOU GOING TO THE COUNTY FAIR TOMORROW?"

"You betcha."

An excruciatingly long silence.

After a few minutes Clyde would get up and say, "Well, how'd ya like a glass of juice?" And then he'd fumble around in the kitchen before emerging with two tiny glasses filled to the brim with grape juice. For the next thirty minutes we'd sit in our rocking chairs, slowly sipping the juice like it was rare Sauvignon. The yelling had made me hoarse, and Clyde had nowhere else to go and nothing else to say, so we'd sit in utter silence. I would spend the next half hour being with Clyde.

At first it drove me nuts. I desperately wanted to say something or do something—read the newspaper, walk around the room or straighten the pictures on his wall. But after a few visits, I started to appreciate our grape-juice-sipping "conversations." In the silent "being-with-ness" of the moment, I started to understand Clyde. I noticed the simplicity of his clothing and the deep serenity of his facial expressions. I studied the photos on his walls. I listened intently to his breathing patterns. I watched his huge hands, the hands that had tossed thousands of hay bales and had tenderly brought food to his wife's mouth. I was soaking in "Clyde-ness." In a strange way, by being with Clyde, I was getting to know Clyde.

That's a picture of contemplative prayer. We get to know Jesus by being with Jesus. That's the agenda, the one thing, of contemplative prayer: being with Jesus. And as we get to know Jesus, our life of service will flow from a deep underground spring of freedom and Christlike wholeness.

Unfortunately, as Thomas Merton once claimed, "There are so

many Christians who have practically no idea of the immense love of God for them, and of the power of that love to do them good. . . . There are thousands of Christians walking about the face of the earth bearing in their bodies the infinite God of whom they know practically nothing."[7] Contemplation immerses us in "the immense love of God" on a daily basis. It's a prayer path that enables us to not only know about God but to experience God.

As a biblical example, Psalm 36:5 declares the intellectual truth about God: "Your love, O LORD, reaches to the heavens, your faithfulness to the skies." Contemplative prayer doesn't bypass our minds; it doesn't just stop at intellectual analysis. And that's exactly what we discover in the next verses of the psalm:

> How *priceless* is your unfailing love!
> Both high and low among men
> *find refuge* in the shadow of your wings.
> They *feast* on the abundance of your house;
> you *give them drink* from your *river of delights.*
> (Psalm 36:7-8, emphasis added)

It involves valuing God, delighting in God, clinging to God, feasting on God's goodness, and drinking from God's river of delight. God isn't just an intellectual concept; God is alive and wants to be known—personally and passionately.

Picture a crisp, clean, glistening green apple. You could identify the precise species, analyze the symmetry of the apple, slice it into eight pieces, examine the seeds under a microscope and note the molecular structure. Or as you analyze the apple, you could pick it up, sink your teeth into it, chew it, taste it, swallow it and enjoy it. Both forms of knowledge are important. But an apple exists to be tasted and digested, not just analyzed. In the same way, God wants us to "taste and see that the LORD is good" (Psalm 34:8).

Would You Please Be Quiet!

Hearing God's heartbeat requires the space of silence. Surprisingly, I learned more about Clyde through the long stretches of silence than I did through a wordy conversation. Being with God, tasting the goodness of God, also involves gobs of silence. The noisy world we live in mutes the beating of God's heart. So although we may try to sit with God, we can't hear the rhythm of his heart, and our lives remain unchanged by the beauty of contemplative prayer.

The solution is simple: find silence. Carve out snatches of silence. Unfortunately, toxic levels of noise fill the spiritual air around us until we don't even notice it anymore. Contemplatives fight for silence like an asthmatic person fights through smog to find pure air. As John Climacus (seventh century) wrote, "Garrulousness [excessive talkativeness] . . . gives rise to boredom, predisposes to lethargy, destroys recollection, distracts attention, obliterates fervor and cuts off prayer. Silence on the other hand is the mother of prayer. It frees the prisoner; it guards the divine flame . . . [and] it protects the sense of penitence."[8]

When I spent a week at St. Procopius Abbey, a Benedictine monastery near Chicago, I joined the brothers in their beautiful rhythm of silence-work-conversation-rest-silence-work-conversation-rest. After our noontime prayer, in which we chanted the psalms, we ate lunch together in deep silence. We passed the bread and soup with eye contact and hand gestures, but we did not speak. As we continued to eat in silence, the words of Scripture that we had just chanted started to work their way into my heart. The beautiful words of the psalms slowly descended deep within me. I discovered the secret of Benedictine spirituality: silence is needed to hear God's heartbeat.

Without the silence, the words of Scripture float on the surface. They cannot descend into my depths. But in the power of the Holy Spirit, the silence allows God's Word to sink in. As I listen to the heartbeat of God, as the silence works within me, God's words of truth and promise and comfort begin to move off the page, filling my eyes, my mind, and then descending into my heart.

As God's heart beats against our chest in the silence, we will often find our prayers growing shorter and more focused. Fourth-century

Christ-followers who left their safe church culture to pursue Jesus in the desert recommended responding to God with short biblical prayers such as "Have mercy on me, O God, according to your unfailing love" (Psalm 51:1) or "Hasten, O God, to save me; O LORD, come quickly to help me" (Psalm 70:1) or "the Jesus Prayer": "Lord Jesus, Son of the Living God, have mercy on me, a sinner."[9] John Climacus claimed that one-word prayers were enough: "Try not to talk excessively in your prayer, in case your mind is distracted by the search for words. . . . Talkative prayer frequently distracts the mind and deludes it, whereas brevity makes for concentration."[10] Short prayers, rooted in a silent being-with-God, quickly begin to sink into the core of our being.

TWO WARNINGS ABOUT THE CONTEMPLATIVE PATH

I mentioned that fifteen years ago I tried contemplative prayer and didn't like it; and it's still hard. As I've ventured down this path over the past fifteen years, I've discovered two fundamental struggles or warnings about praying contemplatively.

First, the practice of silently being with God doesn't always feel good. As we listen to God's heartbeat, we may not feel better. Our brain may not emit endorphins; on the contrary, this path to prayer may fill us with darkness, obscurity and dryness. Teresa of Ávila constantly urged us to jettison expectations about what we should "get" from contemplative prayer: "It is very important that no one be distressed or afflicted over dryness or noisy and distracting thoughts."[11] God may "bless" us with dull prayer experiences. Yes, emotional highs are wonderful, but unlike Martha, we can't demand that Jesus do it our way.

The desert fathers never used contemplative prayer as an escape from struggle. As they prayed, they engaged their inner demons of anger, lust and greed (and they faced some real demons too). It didn't always lead to rapture and delight. In one story a younger brother came to his spiritual father and boasted, "I find myself in peace without an enemy." His spiritual father replied, "Go, beseech God to stir up warfare so that you may regain the affliction that you used to have. For it is by warfare that the soul makes progress."[12] Sometimes contemplative prayer will feel as cozy as sitting in a rocking chair and sipping juice with a friend. On other days it may feel like warfare stirred up inside my soul. Ultimately God controls the results of contemplative prayer.

Second, contemplative prayer remains countercultural. We even live in a culture that's often hostile to contemplative living. Most of us bustle with Martha's efficiency and perpetual productivity—and we're proud of it! This shouldn't surprise us. For hundreds of years we've been shaped and honed by a pragmatic approach to life. *Pragmatism* comes from the Greek word *pragma,* which literally means "business" but also implies efficiency, productivity and practicality.[13] Pragmatism displays a deep impatience with anyone or anything that isn't immediately useful and practical. When pragmatism gets applied to relationships, we tend to say, "People are only as good as the work they do." Unfortunately, this tends to devalue whole groups of people that we label "unproductive"—such as the physically disabled, the emotionally traumatized, the poor, unborn children, the elderly, the sick and the dying..

Pragmatism has a steep price tag. Look at Martha: she's productive and efficient, but she also exudes the toxic fruit of her pragmatic lifestyle. After bulging with anxiety, Martha finally pops and then sprays everyone with her frustration and manipulation. Undiluted pragmatism always leads to manipulation because everything—people, trees, rivers, soil, oceans and even God—becomes an object to manipulate and force into our idea of usefulness. So Martha manipulates others with her harsh and judgmental spirit. She assumes that Jesus doesn't care and that Mary is lazy and unproductive. She manipulates (or attempts to) by demanding that Jesus get with her agenda ("Tell her to help me!"). She manipulates with her compulsivity. Like every other addict in the world, Martha insists that her needs get met right now. Anti-contemplatives never back up and reflect on their lives, how they affect (and sometimes damage) other people and creation. The Marthas of the world have one speed: full speed ahead.

As a result, we live in a culture enamored with "being busy." Schools, sports teams, workplaces and churches (maybe *especially* churches) have conspired to ensure that Martha trumps Mary. According to social commentator David Brooks, the spirit of American culture is known by one quality—energy. "Wherever we are heading," he writes, "we are getting there at great speed and with great energy. It's not the steering wheel that distinguishes us, it's the throttle. . . . The fabric of our lives is frenetic."[14] Brooks also notes that Americans invented the take-out paper coffee cup. We're just too busy to sit down and drink coffee from a porcelain cup like the rest of the world.[15]

Contemplative prayer requires that ordinary people make an extraordinary internal adjustment. Something within us has to stop and say, "Enough! This is crazy! Why am I this busy? Why do I and we constantly ignore Jesus' clear teaching about the 'one thing' that is necessary for us?"[16]

So beginners, like most of us, start down the path of contemplative prayer by making a major adjustment: we start to value "nonbusy," "unproductive" people and activities. For the most part, friendships aren't "productive." Friendships thrive when we practice nonbusyness and linger in each other's presence. Simple, ordinary human activities—displaying compassion, walking beside wounded people, taking time to listen to the hurts or grievances of another human being—require an inefficient squandering of our time and energy. Watching the breeze ripple through the oak leaves in my backyard isn't productive. Most good art—painting and poetry and short stories—isn't efficient. Sabbath time, time with one agenda—being with God and others—isn't productive. Prayer is notoriously unproductive.

As we allow Jesus to train us and shape us, we'll start to value these nonbusy, unproductive activities and things. And as we change our values, we'll change our schedule. If Jesus our Lord and teacher wants to make contemplative prayer the "one thing" that's required of us, then we will make time for it.

ONE PORTRAIT OF LIVING CONTEMPLATIVELY

Of course, this can sound dreadfully abstract if we don't start praying and living more contemplatively. So at some point we have to ask a direct question: How? How do we contemplate? What does contemplative prayer look like? I'm not sure what it would mean for you, but I can tell you what it could mean for me.

Every Tuesday morning, my first deadline looms at 7:40 a.m. when I drive my fifteen-year-old son to high school. Then I usually have fifty minutes before my next appointment. So I rush to Starbucks for my morning cup of coffee. Naturally, I'm in a hurry, so I ask for the paper to-go cup. As I exit Starbucks, I'm tempted to adopt a Martha-like pragmatism: *I must hurry because I'm very busy,* I tell myself. *The items clogging my to-do list cannot wait. The person completing this to-do list [i.e., me] is utterly indispensable. I cannot die or even get sick for a few days. I must produce without slacking.* Pressure? You bet, but that's how a Martha must churn through life.

In spite of the pressure, I resist my Martha mindset of productivity and indispensability so I can find some time alone with God. The desert fathers used to tell their protégés, "Go to your cell, and your cell will teach you everything." In other words, find a specific place for your contemplative practices and then go there. I usually choose the wondrously unproductive "cell" called our local bird sanctuary. The land prices on Long Island are exorbitant. Someone could turn this lucrative outdoor bird zoo into a subdivision for million-dollar homes or offices for orthodontists, but for now it's still a quiet, "useless" space dedicated to bamboo shoots, cardinals, rabbits and a few deer.

So I hold my coffee, Bible and journal, and I sit under an apple tree. As I open my prayer journal to a fresh page, my agenda is simple: Be with God. Spend time with Jesus. Be quiet. Listen. Let the words of the Bible sink deep into my heart. Yes, there's so much to do today. I will get busy, but not yet. So for the next thirty minutes, I'm Mary, sitting at Jesus' feet, listening intently, being with him, knowing him better by being with him.

By 8:30 I'm in the office, and for the next fourteen hours I will jump from one meeting or activity to the next. But if I'm living more contemplatively, listening to Jesus and valuing nonbusy activities, I will discover snatches of time for contemplative prayer. The author Anthony Bloom called them "crumbs of wasted time." He urged us that if we considered the "empty minutes in a day when we will be doing something because we are afraid of emptiness and of being alone with ourselves, we [would] realize that there are plenty of short periods which could belong both to us and to God at the same time."[17]

So I realize that God has been offering me "crumbs of wasted time" throughout the day:

A cancelled appointment at 2:00 p.m.

A few minutes before supper at 5:30 p.m.

A walk across the soccer park at 6:45 p.m. after delivering my son to his practice

A half hour of silence before going to bed at 11:00 p.m.

All of these "crumbs" qualify as "short periods which could belong to [me] and God at the same time."

There's also a communal dimension that could enhance our Mary-path to prayer. On Tuesday nights at our monthly corporate prayer meeting, we often have long gaps between the prayers. These gaps used to annoy me; I wanted someone to fill them with wordy prayers. But what if these gaps are really "crumbs of wasted time" for us to be with God together? What if God is teaching a whole community to enjoy the Mary moments that enter our lives?

Also, on every other Tuesday at our leadership meeting, we've decided to end by 10:00 p.m. We used to roil until near midnight, but we noticed that after 10:00 p.m., we quickly degenerated into a communal, Martha-like, crabby, controlling wrangling. So we said, "Enough!" Now we try to end at 10:00 even if we haven't been productive. After all, why can't we help each other as a community live more contemplatively?

So at 10:30 p.m. I get home on Tuesday nights, bless my sleeping family members, feed the dogs, eat my shredded wheat with bananas and honey, watch a *Seinfeld* rerun and then spend a few more minutes soaking in the presence of Jesus. I usually end my day by walking my dog, Dwight. It's dark and quiet outside, so I have time to listen. I don't force prayers. My only agenda is to be with God. My mind usually scatters and wanders in seventeen directions, but as I walk in the silence, the words that God has spoken into my mind start to descend into my heart. They come alive within me.

WHERE'S THE FRUIT?

It's difficult for us to imagine that contemplative prayer actually does any good. Naturally, there's a balance between contemplation and action. There is an inflow of Jesus' words and an outflow of our service for Jesus. Unfortunately, I've been a pastor for twenty years and one of the saddest scenarios I see is this: sincere men and women who want to serve Jesus, but they don't sit with God in silence until they can hear his heartbeat. Like Martha, they do not contemplate; they only charge full speed ahead and manipulate. Inevitably, they burn out or blow up.

Is there a better way? Yes, it's Mary's path. Jesus said it was the "one thing" necessary for our spiritual lives. But does it do any good? Let's go back to my original questions from fifteen years ago: *What's the point of this? What am I supposed to get out of this? How is this supposed to feed me and help change the world for Jesus' sake? Am I really doing God a favor by snoozing in the woods?*

I keep returning to my all-time favorite contemplative, St. Serafim of Sarov, the Russian equivalent of St. Francis of Assisi. During his lifetime (1759-1833), he spent nearly thirty years in his hermitage deep in the Russian forest, listening to God's heartbeat. But he spent the last twenty years of his life involved in a bustling ministry of counseling, prayer, spiritual direction and healing. Out of his wholeness in Christ, he became a spiritual father to thousands, addressing each person as "my joy" and blessing them with "Christ is risen!"

Jesus' presence poured into him and through him until his words and even his face brought healing to broken lives. The healing wasn't through a program or a strategic plan; it had nothing to do with pragmatism. His contemplative lifestyle allowed him to impact more lives on a deeper level than we do with our frenetic, anxious, manipulative, Martha-like "ministry."

What was his secret? Serafim said, "Acquire a peaceful spirit, and thousands around you will be saved." One of his biographers would ponder, "When he came out of the forest his every word, his every gesture, his very presence was healing to all the people around him. Grace became his second nature." And then the biographer challenges us to ask ourselves: "Out of all the million of words that I have spoken in the course of my life, have I ever managed to speak one—even one, truly healing word to another human being?—pleasant words, yes; kind words, yes; true words, yes. . . . But healing words?"[18]

That is the challenge and the invitation of contemplative prayer. It doesn't disengage us from God and other people. To the contrary, it transforms our vision of the world and then plunges us back into the world. Authentic, Christ-centered contemplatives constantly warn us: "Don't sit with God if you just want time alone. Don't withdraw into your 'cell' if you want to fly into a narcissistic fantasy. If you truly follow Jesus, if you truly spend time with him, you can't abandon the world around you. In reality, your time alone listening to God will also help you listen to the most neglected, suffering, marginal people on this planet. You will be a good Samaritan, but like Serafim, you will serve God from a deep spring of wholeness and goodness and freedom."

So follow Jesus by being with God, hearing his heartbeat of love for you and for the world. With Serafim of Sarov, I want to acquire a peaceful, Christ-filled spirit. And who knows? Maybe one person will be saved.

11

PRAYER AS LOVE

Five years ago my performance (and my approval rating) as a pastor hit an all-time low. It was an ugly scene. The church was torn by factions, gossip, trust issues and worship-war conflicts. Giving and attendance were both plummeting.

In the midst of my clerical nosedive, a respectable older gentleman in the church invited me to lunch. When he asked me how I thought the church was doing, I released my pent-up grief and anger and frustration. "I cannot figure these people out," I protested. "They are driving me nuts. They don't give. They don't show up. They constantly argue about music in our worship services. They don't trust me. I tell you, it's enough to make me quit."

My friend quietly listened to all my complaints, interrupting only to ask a few pointed questions, and then he continued listening. After I had vented for thirty minutes, he looked at me and said, "So why do you think people are acting this way? Why don't they trust you?" *Why don't they trust me?* I thought. *That makes it sound like it's my problem. Um, this sounds like a setup.* I declined to answer the question and put it back on him: "Beats me. Why do *you* think they don't trust me?"

He paused, cleared his throat and then quietly said, "You have a teenager, right? What would happen if you constantly chided and scolded him without ever praising or affirming him? Would he like it?"

"No."

"Exactly," he replied, "You see, your teenager would have to feel secure first. He needs to know that no matter what he does, you'll still love and accept him. Matt, people won't trust you until they know that you love them. Love is the critical issue here. It's not about your preaching or the worship music. It's all about relationships. And relationships boil down to one thing: love."

As I reflect on that painful but fruitful conversation, I realize that my friend gave me a good definition for the entire Christian life: it all boils down to love. That's also a good summary for our prayer lives. God is love. Prayer connects us to God. As we connect with God, God teaches us to love others. Love moves us to pray for others, and praying for others is the best way to love them. When I don't pray for others, I am failing at love. As St. Augustine said nearly seventeen hundred years ago, "True, whole prayer is nothing but love."[1] So, practically speaking, the simple question of "How can I pray for you?" may be one of the most loving things I can do for you.

PRAYER: A COLOSSAL COP-OUT?

Honestly, that's not the way I usually look at prayer. Actually praying for others often becomes my last-ditch option. So when I have no idea what to do for Bob, if I don't really want to be with Bob, I can always ask him, "Hey, Bob, how can I pray for you?" That one-liner usually absolves me of loving Bob. And the next time I see Bob, I'll recall my original question as I quickly pray, "Dear God, bless Bob." Than I can wave and smile and tell Bob, "Hey, Bob, I've been praying for you!"[2] Sadly, the question "How can I pray for you?" usually means nothing.

Most of us don't see a direct connection between love and prayer. Sure, it's nice to pray for others, but *real* love means doing things for people, and prayer isn't a "thing." So if a man is hungry, I should give him something, like a turkey sandwich. If I love kids, I should do something for them, like taking a slot in my church's nursery schedule. These things get my blood pumping with the oxygen of real love. By comparison, prayer seems anemic because it's not "something." It's like offering a hungry man an empty plate. Maybe my prayers are an evasion of love or even a colossal cop-out.

I've wrestled with the prayer-as-an-evasion charge partially because I've used prayer to neglect people. I pray therefore I am ignoring you. Thankfully, as I read the Bible, it constantly reminds me that prayer isn't a quick and painless way to evade love. To the contrary, prayer is a "thing." As a demonstration of love, it's as real as a turkey sandwich. So if I love you, I will pray for you. Prayer leads to love. Prayer is a relationship of love.

So when I ask that simple question—"How can I pray for you?"—it may have more power and significance than I ever imagined. When I regularly ask you that question, listening for your response and then praying for you, it becomes a radical, heart-changing act of love.

PRAYER CREATES LOVING RELATIONSHIPS

How does that question change our lives? When my friend sat me down and helped me bring my life back to love, God started to change the course of my life. I had made life about so many others things—success, pleasure, comfort. Love was certainly in the mix, but love wasn't at the center of it all. Since then, over the past few years, through God's gracious work despite my sin, God has been teaching me that life really does boil down to loving relationships.

In his gripping and moving book, *The Boy Who Was Raised as a Dog,* child psychiatrist Dr. Bruce Perry shares the stories of severely traumatized children. In one of his cases a young boy named Justin was left with his grandmother, but when she died, her live-in boyfriend named Arthur tried to care for him. But since Arthur didn't have any experience raising children, he used his natural skills as a dog breeder to care for Justin. So he treated Justin just like one of his dogs, putting him in a cage most of the day, letting him out to eat and urinate.

Amazingly, as Dr. Perry shares these heart-wrenching stories, he also expresses hope for healing of the traumatic memories. But Perry is clear about how the healing will take place—in and through loving relationships: "The more healthy relationships a child has, the more likely he will be to recover from trauma and thrive. Relationships are the agents of change and the most powerful therapy is human love. . . . Recovery from trauma and neglect is all about relationships—rebuilding trust, regaining confidence, returning to a sense of security and reconnecting to love." While he acknowledges the importance of medication and therapy, he also concludes that "all the children who ultimately thrived following our treatment did so because of a strong social network that surrounded and supported them."[3]

How do we develop more healthy relationships so we can thrive? The Christian answer starts here: pray for others. I can keep asking you that simple question: "How can I pray for you?" Then as I listen and pray for you, I'm helping to create powerful relationships of love. Prayer isn't an evasion of love; prayer releases love, and then love flows back into prayer.

The apostle Paul noticed this prayer-love and love-prayer connection. For him, prayer isn't a cop-out; instead, prayer and love dwell in a rich spiritual symbiosis. They need each other and feed off each other. Notice how often Paul unites prayer with relationships of love:

> "First, I thank my God through Jesus Christ for all of you. . . . God . . . is my witness how constantly I remember you in my prayers." (Romans 1:8-10)

> "In all my prayers for all of you, I always pray with joy. . . . I have you in my heart." (Philippians 1:4, 7)

> "We always thank God, the Father of our Lord Jesus Christ, when we pray for you." (Colossians 1:3)

> "We always thank God for all of you, mentioning you in our prayers. . . . For we know, brothers loved by God, that he has chosen you." (1 Thessalonians 1:2, 4)

> "I thank God, whom I serve, . . . as night and day I constantly

remember you in my prayers. Recalling your tears, I long to see you, so that I may be filled with joy." (2 Timothy 1:3-4)

From a Christian viewpoint this makes sense because the God who designed us for relationships of love also exists as a relationship of love. God isn't a solitary monarch perched on top of his cosmic throne. God is a loving community of Father, Son and Holy Spirit. Even the names of the Trinity suggest relationship and love. God relates within God. God communicates within God. As Michael Downey writes, "Christian faith is Trinitarian faith. Christian life is Trinitarian life. And Christian spirituality is Trinitarian spirituality."[4] I would add that Christian prayer is trinitarian prayer.

This has radically altered my approach to prayer. Now, as a follower of Jesus, whenever I ask you, "How can I pray for you?" and then I really do it, I'm not starting a new prayer dialogue with God; I'm merely joining God's communal prayer of love for you. The Trinity constantly prays; when we pray, we join in God's communal dance of love. The Father's heart beats for you; Jesus, the Son, intercedes for you; the Holy Spirit woos and convicts you. They were at the "prayer meeting" long before I ever showed up with my request.

Prayer immerses us in God's ongoing community of love. Jean Vanier tells a moving story about Peter, one of the members of his L'Arche communities, a young man with Down syndrome. Peter loved to talk to and about Jesus. When somebody asked him what he did when he prayed, Peter replied, "I listen." Then when he was asked what God says to him, Peter looked up and said, "He just says, 'You are my beloved son.'"[5]

That's the essence of intercessory prayer: we are immersed in God's ongoing relationship of love. So every time I pray for specific prayer requests—your biopsy, your upcoming MCAT exams, your need for a job or healing after a divorce—a miracle takes place: I take you by the hand and lead you (against your will even!) into the presence of the living God. As we pray for each other, we unite together in love and walk together into God's love for us.

PRAYER EXPOSES MY HEART

On one level I have to object to what I just wrote: it could make it sound too easy. Just pray for others, and every relationship will be awash in love? If that's true, then why doesn't prayer always produce pure love between people? Why do we pray and still fail at love? Sadly (but also hopefully), I've been learning another profound truth about prayer as love: as I pray for you, as I hear the triune God whisper into my heart and your heart the words "You are my beloved child," I realize that I don't love like God. As a matter of fact, I'm very conflicted about loving others. I love and I hate. I forgive you and then resent you. I'm long-suffering and impatient. I'm kind and rude. I'm courageous and insecure. Prayer also exposes the depths of sin in my heart.

Jean Vanier said that as soon as he started living with the severely disabled, trying to love them and pray for them, he discovered the hardness of his heart. His friends with disabilities were crying out for love, but he couldn't give it. "At particular moments of stress," he confessed, "I saw forces of hate rising up within me, and the capacity to hurt someone who was weak and was provoking me. That, I think, was what caused me the most pain: to discover who I really am, and to realize that maybe I did not want to know who I really was!"[6]

I have a strong pull to deny this part of myself. Sure, you can call me a "sinner" in the abstract, but please don't label me a real sinner and then list my specific sins. To name my sins one by one, listing the concrete ways that I've failed at love, overwhelms my heart with terror and shame.

But as I pray for you, as I immerse you in God's love for you and me, I will face the inadequacy of my love. My love is inadequate because I'm finite, but I also fail at love because I'm sinful. I have such a strong pull to focus my life on me, but prayer really is all about you and your needs. Like Jean Vanier said, as I try to love you, as I try to pray for you and focus only on you, it moves me to profound humility. But when I ask you, "How can I pray for you?" I also commit myself to do nothing out of selfish conceit, looking not just to my interests but to your interests (see Philippians 2:3-4). In other words, intercessory prayer isn't an evasion of love. By focusing on you in prayer, God slowly retrains my stubborn, self-centered heart so I can love you better.

PRAYER REMOVES MY JUDGMENTS

In particular, praying for you purifies my heart by burning away the dross of my judgmental, exclusive spirit. Every culture, every group, every family, every person seems to develop unique ways to judge and exclude others. Anthropologist Mary Douglas provides one example from the Nuer tribe of East Africa: "When a monstrous birth occurs [i.e., any kind of 'deformed' child], the defining lines between humans and animals may be threatened. . . . So the Nuer treat monstrous births as baby hippopotamuses, accidentally born to humans, and with this labeling, the appropriate action is clear. They gently lay them in the river where they belong."[7]

As barbaric as this sounds, I wonder how often I judge and exclude other human beings. Who do we treat like baby hippos, gently placing them in the river so we don't have to care for them? I'm thankful for some loving, courageous friends who are teaching me to see the people that we often exclude from our midst. My friend Rich started a ministry through our church for children whose fathers are in prison. Another dear friend runs a ministry for women who have been sexually abused. When my friend Jim brought me to that abandoned parking lot (see chapter nine), I was shocked to see a line of homeless people streaming in from the surrounding woods—I didn't know we had any homeless folks in our posh Long Island community. Every Sunday my little friend Adriel, a ten-year-old boy with Down syndrome, runs into my arms and hugs me as he calls me "Big Daddy!"

The poor, the imprisoned (or their family members), the abused, the homeless, those with disabilities, the moral failures, the addicts—these are just some of the people we tend to judge and then exclude from our midst. We want them to remain invisible. But something remarkable happens when we pray for the excluded and the invisible:

we see them. It's very difficult to pray for someone and then to exclude them. As we pray for these invisible people, we notice them and they matter to us. Once we start praying for them, we'll slowly start to see and love them as God sees and loves them.

Our church leadership team developed a very simple method for providing pastoral care to our congregation: we divided the church directory into nine sections, and then we started praying for everyone. We debated if we should add something else—make a phone call, send an e-mail, write a note—but we decided to stick with the basic prayer plan. Just pray for everyone regularly and consistently.

Speaking for myself, the results were remarkable. As I pondered the question of "How can I pray for them?" I started to notice people. I paid attention to their families and jobs, their spiritual lives and fears and pain. I had to notice these things. As a result, we started to know our people on a much deeper level.

Simone Weil claims that our attention to God (i.e., our prayer lives) will make us attentive to others. So she urges us to give our loving attention to everyone God brings into our lives, especially the confused and troubled. But according to Weil, this isn't easy, for "to give one's attention to a sufferer is a very rare and difficult thing; it is almost a miracle; it *is* a miracle."[8] Instead we tend to lump people into categories without truly paying attention to the unique "other" before us. But invisible, excluded, judged people don't need our analysis or even our "ministry efforts"; they just need us to notice them, to see them, to give them our attention.

Jesus was the master noticer. He saw ragged people that everyone else wanted to shun and ignore. And then he challenged us to notice those we normally exclude. On one occasion, Jesus confronted a religious leader named Simon who was shunning a woman described as having "lived a sinful life" (Luke 7:37). "Do you see this woman?" Jesus asked Simon (Luke 7:44). Of course he saw her. No, Jesus meant, do you *really* see her? Do you notice her? Are you giving your full, loving, warm attention to this broken but beautifully redeemed human being?

That's why Jesus insisted that we pray for our enemies. If you hurt me, I'll want to exclude you from my life. But once I start praying for you, you start sneaking back into my heart again. I can't help it because I've lifted you into the presence of the triune God. Prayer brings us to the center of the Trinity's great redemptive work: the cross. At the cross Father, Son and Holy Spirit united to display costly, creative and redemptive love for the world. At the cross I was reconciled to the Father, through the work of the Son, in the power of the Spirit, who makes me a new creation. So when I pray for you, I stand with you at the foot of the cross. I don't have a shred of moral superiority over you. I can't judge you, demean you or exclude you. We are both flawed and broken sinners, desperate for God's grace.

THE POWER OF OUR POWERLESSNESS

Perhaps the hardest thing about praying for you is that it just feels so powerless. In contrast, when I can do something practical for you—rake your yard, edit your letter, buy your lunch—I feel powerful; I feel in control. For instance, a few years ago I learned to cook. It's almost as if the world—including my own mother—had conspired to keep this skill from me. But I discovered that I could actually follow a recipe and make something. In my tiny circle of influence, I'm famous for making large pots of mulligatawny or African peanut soup (with huge scoops of chunky peanut butter). I love the excitement of watching people eat my amazing creations. I feel so powerful and useful. (Okay, so it wasn't like I made a log cabin or strangled a cougar with my bare hands. But I did make *something*, and now my friends aren't hungry anymore.)

By comparison, prayer feels powerless. I suppose at times prayer gets charged with power. The Bible is filled with examples of prayer power. And I've certainly witnessed the power of prayer in my life and in the lives of others. But most of the time prayer appears so quiet, small, hidden, slow and even weak. That's the real "folly" of prayer that this book has explored over and over again. Honestly, on some days making soup seems more useful than spending time at a prayer meeting.

I used to resist this unpleasant truth about prayer. How can God do anything through such a weak, frail, useless instrument called prayer? It's so wrapped up with humans, and humans are notoriously slow and vulnerable. A colony of bacteria can kill us. A lustful desire can drive us insane with addiction. And then we're also stubborn, spiritually inattentive and even callous toward God and others. How can God possibly use our prayers to do anything for good in this world? It just seems so powerless.

However, I'm starting to notice how God works through our powerlessness and our weakness (not to mention our pain and our failures) to accomplish his purposes for the world. The Bible contains so many stories and images of God's ability and even delight to use small, weak things and people: Gideon and his tiny army equipped with pickle pots; David, the youngest son, and his inconsistent saint-sinner track record; the promised Messiah, who came through a shattered remnant of God's people; Jesus, the Son of God, born in a cattle stall, steaming with hot blood and bile; Jesus' presence, which appears in such unlikely places, like bread and wine and that motley thing called the church. It's all so quirky and comical. But it's something woven into the universe. God made it that way. He even redeemed us from death and sin and hell by sending Jesus to die on a cross. Now that's the real power of the powerless.

So here's what I'm learning about prayer as an act of love: sometimes the best way to love you is to be powerless. Yes, at times I should get off my duff and make you a sandwich or work for fair housing or fight against world hunger. But sometimes I can't fix you or your problems. I can't change you or your circumstances. But I can be with you in your powerlessness, and I can allow God to be with both of us as we pray.

It's interesting that the New Testament uses the Greek word *dynamis,* or "power," forty-one times, but it's often combined with the word *asthenia,* or "weakness." Power and weakness are linked like prayer and love. God longs to plant and cultivate real strength in us, but it often grows in the soil of our weakness. This God of power wants to pour his strength into broken human recipients, empowering us to live with love and courage and joy and gratitude and endurance. But God only pours his power into empty hands. When he finds us preoccupied with our own strength and cleverness, he won't give us what we don't want.[9]

I'm actually starting to enjoy this aspect of prayer. In my youthful arrogance, I assumed that I could fix things for people. I assumed that I was in control of every situation: just follow the recipe, and I'll have a pot of solutions. Unfortunately, in my "strength" I often didn't really help people. I couldn't be present with people in their pain and suffering. I wanted to do something for them, and quite often it wasn't the "something" that they really needed.

Now in my weakness and helplessness I'm learning to come to God with you and for you. Sometimes all we can do is admit that we're powerless. Then we offer up our weak and seemingly useless prayers. And God hears us, and God comes through our weakness to give us his power.

I think of my friend Maggie, who experienced a dark, dark night of the soul. After finding the man of her dreams, she dropped into the abyss of a deep depression. Everything went dark in her mind and her body. Three years ago I would have had plenty of answers and solutions for her. I would have been so clever and powerful. But now all I could do was to sit with her in her pain. We prayed. I didn't know what to do, didn't have any answers, so I said, "Maggie, I have no idea what to say, so could we just read Psalm 77." Then I read Psalm 77, an agonizing psalm of lament, and I went home. I left feeling utterly powerless.

The next week another leader of our church visited with Maggie. She was still suffering intensely, but when the leader asked if he could pray for her, Maggie said, "Yes, but before you pray, please read Psalm 77. I've been clinging to it all week. It's my lifeline to God." Apparently when we read Psalm 77 in utter powerlessness, God showed up in her life with power.

At times the best, most powerful and most useful way to love you is to get to the end of myself. I admit that I can't fix you or change you. My soup or my advice or my words won't heal your brokenness. But I can be with you, and we can go together to the Father. So we come as weak and frail and hardhearted instruments, but we also come as sons and daughters who know their Father's heart. And on your behalf I do something so useless that leads to such power: I pray for you.

So when I pray for you and when you pray for me, it is powerful. It is ministry. It is healing. It is "our invincible weapon."[10] It is a radical and even a countercultural act of love. Genuine, heartfelt prayer—not just given as an excuse or a last resort—is the balm that heals our broken world. Prayer is an act of rebellion against the status quo. It's an act of loving subversion against loneliness, hate, indifference and coldness.

So the next time I ask someone, "How can I pray for you?" I won't ask it glibly. True, whole prayer is nothing but love. True, whole prayer can change the world.

CONCLUSION

PRAYER AS PRAYING

It's my hope that you will not only read this book, but that you will actually walk down each prayer path by praying. Søren Kierkegaard once told a humorous parable about a swimming coach who constantly exhorted his team to swim better and faster. He yelled and screamed and offered swimming instructions. He stood on the side of the pool and flapped his arms to demonstrate the correct technique. The coach excelled in his vast knowledge about swimming. The only problem was that he couldn't swim. Actually, he had never stepped into water that went over his head.[1]

In the same way, Kierkegaard urged followers of Jesus not just to talk about prayer and to help others pray; he wanted us to start praying. Right now. So my advice is this: don't just stand at the side of the pool—dive in. Get wet. Flap around in the water if you must, but at least jump into the pool.

Or in terms of the eleven paths to prayer in this book:

Go ahead and groan toward God.
Taste the bread and drink the wine.
Cry out to God.

Enjoy the mystery of God.
Enter the dark night of the soul.
Start an argument with God.
Take a long, slow journey through prayer.
Invoke the wild but good name of Jesus.
Start paying attention.
Feel God's heartbeat.
And love deeply, embracing sinners and enemies.

But the important thing is to pray. You can't pray by reading about it or thinking about it or even telling others about it. You can only pray by praying. So my prayer for you is that you will make time for prayer. And even when you can't use words, you can still groan or you can still listen for God's heartbeat of love. You can still cry out to God in the midst of trouble. And that's your prayer. So God will listen and respond.

NOTES

Chapter 1: Prayer as Guttural Groaning

[1]See C. S. Lewis's description of our future glory in his essay "The Weight of Glory," in *The Weight of Glory* (San Francisco: HarperSanFrancisco, 2001), pp. 25-46.

[2]Adapted from Franz Wright, *Walking to Martha's Vineyard* (New York: Alfred A. Knopf, 2003), p. 73.

[3]Blaise Pascal, *Pensées* (Baltimore: Penguin Books, 1968), p. 169. Pascal also observed, "Misery—the only thing which consoles us for our miseries is diversion, and yet this is the greatest of our miseries. For it is this which principally hinders us from reflecting upon ourselves and which makes us insensibly ruin ourselves. Without this we should be in a state of weariness, and this weariness should spur us to seek a more solid means of escaping it. But diversion amuses us, and leads us unconsciously to death."

[4]This shouldn't turn Christ-followers into whiners and complainers. Whining and complaining often focus on just me and my situation. Stemming from self-pity, whining makes our world narrow and small. Groaning stems from a hope in God that makes our world broad and large. Groaning ushers us into God's larger story of redemption. Yes, the world is broken, but through his life, death and resurrection, Jesus is healing us and his fallen creation. But it still hurts and aches, and others hurt as well. So as I enter into this cosmic groaning, it broadens my world by making me less self-focused and more compassionate.

[5]Judith Herman, *Trauma and Recovery* (New York: Basic Books, 1992), p. 1.

[6]Condensed from Bruce D. Perry and Maia Szalavitz, *The Boy Who Was Raised as a Dog: And Other Stories from a Child Psychologist's Notebook: What Traumatized Children Can Teach Us About Loss, Love and Healing* (Cambridge, Mass.: Basic Books, 2006), pp. 92-95.

[7]Peter Brown, *Augustine of Hippo* (Berkeley: University of California Press, 1969), p. 156.

[8]Augustine, quoted in ibid., p. 157.

[9]Joe Bayly, quoted in H. Norman Wright, *Recovering from the Losses of Life* (Grand Rapids: Revell, 2000) p. 189.

Chapter 2: Prayer as Skin, Trees, Blood, Bread and Wine

[1]"Sacrament" derives from the Latin term *sacramentum,* which derives from the New Testament Greek word *mysterion.* This Greek word refers to the deep mystery of God's plan to save us in and through Jesus Christ (see, for example, Ephesians 3:2-12, where Paul mentions the word four times). The New Testament does not connect it with what we call the sacraments (e.g., the Lord's Supper). However, we do know that early in church history, theologians like Tertullian and Augustine utilized baptism and Eucharist, water and bread and wine, as sacraments that conveyed the *mysterion* of the good news of salvation. See Alister McGrath, *Christian Theology* (Malden, Mass.: Blackwell, 1997), p. 495.

[2]Hans Urs von Balthasar, ed., *The Scandal of the Incarnation: Irenaeus Against the Heresies*, trans. John Saward (San Francisco: Ignatius, 1981), p. 1.

[3]"'So-called gnosis' was an enormous temptation in the early Christian church. By contrast, persecution, even the bloodiest, posed far less of a threat to the Church's continuing purity and further development. Gnosticism had its roots in late antiquity, drew on oriental and Jewish sources, and multiplied into innumerable esoteric doctrines and sects. Then, like a vampire, the parasite took hold of the youthful bloom and vigour of Christianity. What made it so insidious was the fact that the Gnostics very often did not want to leave the Church. Instead, they claimed to be offering a superior and more authentic exposition of Holy Scripture, though, of course, this was only for 'superior souls'; the common folk were left to get on with their crude practices" (ibid.).

[4]Following C. S. Lewis in his *Mere Christianity* (New York: Macmillan, 1977), I'm using this phrase in its theological sense—i.e., Gnosticism isn't just an innocent alternative to Christian spirituality but a defective heresy that stands under God's judgment and damnation. In Paul's words, it represents "a different gospel" (Galatians 1:6-9).

[5]See Pablo Neruda, *Selected Odes of Pablo Neruda*, trans. Margaret Sayers Peden (Berkeley: University of California Press, 1990), pp. 325-27.

[6]Balthasar, *Scandal of the Incarnation,* p. 17.

[7]Ibid., p. 9.

[8]Lewis, *Mere Christianity,* p. 65.

[9]John Calvin, quoted in Leonard J. Vander Zee, *Christ, Baptism and the Lord's Supper* (Downers Grove, Ill.: InterVarsity Press, 2004), p. 57.

[10]Quoted in ibid., p. 68.

[11]Robert Louis Wilken, *The Spirit of Early Christian Thought: Seeking the Face of God* (New Haven, Conn.: Yale University Press, 2003), p. 27.

[12]Ronald Rolheiser, *The Holy Longing* (New York: Doubleday, 1999), p. 90.

[13]Rolheiser, *Holy Longing,* pp. 84-85.

[14]Wendell Berry, *Sex, Economy, Freedom & Community* (New York: Pantheon Books, 1992), p. 103. Berry continues this line of thought by adding (correctly, I believe) that this view of the Bible and creation has profound implications for our stewardship of the earth. "It is clearly impossible to assign holiness exclusively to the built church without denying holiness to the rest of Creation, which is then said to be 'secular.' The world, which God looked at and found entirely good, we find none too good to pollute entirely and destroy piecemeal. The church, then, becomes a kind of preserve of 'holiness,' from which certified lovers of God assault and plunder the 'secular' earth. Not only does this repudiate God's approval of His work; it refuses also to honor the Bible's explicit instruction to regard the works of the Creation as God's revelation of Himself."

[15]Quoted in Andreas Andreopoulos, *The Sign of the Cross: The Gesture, the Mystery, the History* (Brewster, Mass.: Paraclete Press, 2006), p. xi.

Chapter 3: Prayer as Desperation

[1]Tim Jones, *The Art of Prayer* (Colorado Springs: Waterbrook, 2005), p. 13.

[2]Ibid., pp. 16-17.

[3]Blaise Pascal, *Pensées* (Baltimore: Penguin Books, 1966), pp. 88, 95.

[4]James Weldon Johnson, *God's Trombones* (New York: Penguin Books, 1981), p. 13.

[5]James L. Kugel, *The God of Old* (New York: Free Press, 2003), p. 110.

Chapter 4: Prayer as Mystery

[1]Kathleen Norris, *The Cloister Walk* (New York: Riverhead Books, 1996), p. 97.

[2]Ibid., p. 92.

[3]Quoted in Jeremy Campbell, *The Many Faces of God: Science's 400-Year Quest for Images of the Divine* (New York: W. W. Norton, 2006), p. 259.

[4]Jerry Sittser, *When God Doesn't Answer Your Prayers* (Grand Rapids: Zondervan, 2007), p. 142.

Chapter 5: Prayer as Absence

[1]These words were spoken by the eighteenth-century English reformer John Wesley.

[2]Summarized from David Van Biema, "Mother Teresa's Crisis of Faith," *Time*, August 23, 2007 <www.time.com/time/world/article/0,8599,1655415,00.html>.

[3]Iain Matthew, *The Impact of God: Soundings from St. John of the Cross* (London: Hodder & Stoughton, 1995), p. 11.

[4]From "The Spiritual Canticle," quoted in Kieran Kavanaugh, *John of the Cross: Doctor of Light and Love* (New York: Crossroad, 1999), p. 15.

[5]Quoted in Matthew, *Impact of God*, p. 25.

[6]Quoted in Kavanaugh, *John of the Cross*, pp. 109-12.

[7]From "The Living Flame of Love," quoted in ibid., p. 33.

[8]Quoted in ibid., pp. 61, 115.

[9]Matthew, *Impact of God*, p. 80.

[10]Quoted in Kavanaugh, *John of the Cross*, p. 91.

[11]Ibid., p. 91.

[12]Ibid., p. 86.

Chapter 6: Prayer as an Argument with God

[1]Judith Kunst, *The Burning Word* (Brewster, Mass.: Paraclete Press, 2006), pp. 39-40.

[2]Anson Laytner, *Arguing with God* (Northvale, N.J.: Jason Aronson, 1990), p. xv.

[3]Ibid., p. 184.

[4]Quoted in Michele Novotni and Randy Petersen, *Angry with God* (Colorado Springs: NavPress, 2001), p. 32.

[5]Quoted in Laytner, *Arguing with God*, p. 223.

[6]This is my own revised version of a short drama titled "The Long Silence." As far as I know, the original author is unknown. I found the original version in John Stott, *The Cross of Christ* (Downers Grove, Ill.: InterVarsity Press, 1986), pp. 336-37.

Chapter 7: Prayer as a Long, Slow Journey

[1]Quoted in Sue Monk Kidd, *When the Heart Waits* (San Francisco: HarperSanFrancisco, 1992), p. 21.

[2]David Baily Harned, *Patience: How We Wait upon the World* (Lantham, Md.: Cowley Publications, 1997), p. 7.

[3]An insightful and funny study about kvetching—and Yiddish language and culture—is found in Michael Wex, *Born to Kvetch: Yiddish Language and Culture in All of Its Moods* (New York: Harper Perennial, 2006).

[4]Kosuke Koyama, *Three Mile an Hour God: Biblical Reflections* (Maryknoll, N.Y.: Orbis, 1980), pp. 6-7.

[5]Noelle Oxenhandler, "Fall from Grace: How Modern Life Has Made Waiting a Desperate Act," *The New Yorker,* June 16, 1997, p. 65.

[6]Harned, *Patience,* p. 44.

[7]Quoted in Thomas H. Green, *When the Well Runs Dry* (Notre Dame, Ind.: Ave Maria Press, 1979), p. 113.

[8]Harned, *Patience,* p. 158.

[9]Koyama, *Three Mile an Hour God,* p. 7.

[10]For an overview of how our emotions (including anger) connect with the spiritual life, see Peter Scazzero's fine book *Emotionally Healthy Spirituality: Unleash the Power of Authentic Life in Christ* (Nashville: Integrity Publishers, 2006).

[11]Romano Guardini, *The Virtues: On Forms of Moral Life,* trans. Stella Lange (Chicago: Regnery, 1967), p. 34.

[12]Ibid., p. 35.

Chapter 8: Prayer as a Dangerous Activity

[1]C. S. Lewis, *Mere Christianity* (San Francisco: HarperSanFrancisco, 1980), p. 202.

[2]Thomas Cahill, *The Gifts of the Jews: How a Tribe of Desert Nomads Changed the Way Everyone Thinks and Feels* (New York: Nan A. Talese, 1998), p. 63.

[3]Belden Lane, *The Solace of Fierce Landscapes: Exploring Desert and Mountain Spirituality* (New York: Oxford University Press, 1998), pp. 44-46.

[4]Flannery O'Connor, "A Good Man Is Hard to Find," *Collected Works* (New York: Library of America, 1988), p. 152.

[5]Quoted in Rick Baas, *The Book of Yaak* (Boston: Houghton Mifflin, 1996), p. 68.

[6]John Webster, *Holiness* (Grand Rapids: Eerdmans, 2003), pp. 50-51.

[7]Quoted in Lane, *Solace of Fierce Landscapes,* p. 62.

[8]See ibid., pp. 62-78. In the history of Christian spirituality, this negative way (also called the apophatic tradition) reminds us of our utter poverty to fully capture God with our analysis and intellectual categories. This tradition should run parallel with the more affirming tradition (also called the kataphatic, or "speaking according to" tradition). Both traditions are necessary because one can serve as a check to the other.

[9]J. R. R. Tolkien, *The Hobbit* (New York: Ballantine Books, 1980), p. 18.

Chapter 9: Prayer as Paying Attention

[1]Emilie Griffin, *Doors into Prayer* (Brewster, Mass.: Paraclete Press, 2001), p. 22.

[2]Thomas Merton, *Thoughts in Solitude* (New York: Farrar, Straus & Giroux, 1958), p. 39.

[3]Quoted in Thomas de Zengotita, "The Numbing of the American Mind: Culture as Anesthetic," *Harper's Magazine,* April 2002, pp. 33-34.

[4]Louise Story, "Product Packages Now Shout to Get Your Attention," *New York Times,* August 10, 2007.

[5]Denise Levertov, *The Stream and the Sapphire* (New York: New Directions Books, 1997), p. 15.

[6]C. S. Lewis, *The Problem of Pain* (New York: Macmillan, 1977), p. 93.

[7]This is a paraphrase of what I remember from a lecture I heard on one of Rohr's CDs.

[8]Richard Rohr, *Adam's Return* (New York: Crossroad, 2004), pp. 35, 38.

[9]Simone Weil, *Waiting for God* (New York: Perennial Classics, 2001), pp. 57-65.

[10]"One who really meditates does not merely think, he also loves, and by his love he enters into that reality and knows it so to speak from within, by a kind of identification" (Thomas Merton, *Spiritual Direction and Meditation* [Collegeville, Minn.: Order of St. Benedict, Inc., 1960], p. 52).

[11]Søren Kierkegaard, "For Self-Examination and Judge for Yourself," quoted at <www.hebrew4christians.com/Articles/Love_Letter/love_letter.html>. Accessed January 2, 2009.

[12]Franz Wright, *God's Silence* (New York: Alfred A. Knopf, 2006), p. 8.

[13]Here's the quote I read: "You are not normal. If you are reading these pages, you probably belong to the minority of the world's population that has a

steady job, adequate access to social security, and enjoys substantial political freedom. Moreover, you live on more than $2 a day, and, unlike 860 million others, you can read. The percentage of humanity that combines all of these attributes is minuscule. . . . Statistically, a 'normal' human being in today's world is poor, lives in oppressive physical, social, and political conditions, and is ruled by an unresponsive and corrupt government" (Moises Naim, "Dangerously Unique," *Foreign Policy,* September/October, 2005, p. 122).

[14]This pattern is loosely based on a pattern of Ignatian prayer called the prayer of examen. For more information on this simple but profound way to practice prayer-pondering, see Richard Foster, *Prayer: Finding the Heart's True Home* (San Francisco: HarperSanFrancisco, 1992); Timothy Gallagher, *The Examen Prayer* (New York: Crossroad, 2006).

Chapter 10: Prayer as Feeling God's Heartbeat

[1]I have made a few minor changes to this story, which I first read in Ronald Rolheiser, *Forgotten Among the Lilies* (New York: Doubleday, 2005), p. 175.

[2]Teresa of Ávila, *The Autobiography of St. Teresa of Ávila* (New York: One Spirit, 1995), p. 44.

[3]Thomas Merton, *Contemplative Prayer* (Garden City, N.Y.: Image Books, 1971), p. 29.

[4]Saint Nonnus (fourth century), quoted in Belden Lane, *The Solace of Fierce Landscapes: Exploring Desert and Mountain Spirituality* (New York: Oxford University Press, 1998), p. 199.

[5]Attributed to Gregory the Great (sixth century), quoted in Lane, *Solace of Fierce Landscapes.*

[6]Anthony Bloom, *Beginning to Pray* (Ramsey, N.J.: Paulist Press, 1970), p. 94.

[7]Thomas Merton, *What Is Contemplation?* (Springfield, Ill.: Templegate, 1978), pp. 7, 17.

[8]Quoted in Thomas Spidlik, *Drinking from the Hidden Fountain* (Kalamazoo, Mich.: Cistercian Publications, 1994), p. 137.

[9]See my book *Holy Fools: Following Jesus with Reckless Abandon* (Carol Stream, Ill.: Tyndale House, SaltRiver Press, 2008).

[10]Quoted in Lane, *Solace of Fierce Landscapes,* p. 200.

[11]Teresa, *Autobiography,* p. 119.

[12]John Chryssavgis, *In the Heart of the Desert* (Bloomington, Ind.: World Wisdom, 2003), p. 60.

[13]This is developed further in Ronald Rolheiser, *The Shattered Lantern: Rediscovering a Felt Presence of God* (New York: Crossroad, 2001), pp. 37-42.

[14]David Brooks, *On Paradise Drive: How We Live Now (and Always Have) in the Future Tense* (New York: Simon & Schuster, 2004), p. 75.

[15]Research over the past twenty years indicates that American children are more harried and busier than ever. Based on this research, David Brooks concludes, "In short, the childhood of unsupervised loitering, wandering, exploring has been replaced by the childhood of adult-supervised improvement. Bike riding around town has given way to oboe lessons and SAT prep. Time spent hanging out on the corner is now spent in the backseat of the van, going from after-school tutoring to community service" (ibid., p. 142).

[16]If you need some help crying "Enough!" consider these words from Thomas Merton: "Blinded by their desire for ceaseless motion, for a constant sense of achievement . . . they work themselves into a state in which they cannot believe that they are pleasing God unless they are busy with a dozen jobs at the same time. Sometimes they fill the air with lamentations and complain that they no longer have any time for prayer, but they have become such experts in deceiving themselves that they do not realize how insincere their lamentations are. They not only allow themselves to be involved in more and more work, they actually go looking for new jobs. And the busier they become the more mistakes they make" (*The Inner Experience: Notes on Contemplation* [San Francisco: HarperSanFrancisco, 2003], p. 209).

[17]Bloom, *Beginning to Pray,* p. 81.

[18]Julia de Beausobre, *Flame in the Snow* (Springfield, Ill.: Templegate, 1996), pp. xii-xiii.

Chapter 11: Prayer as Love

[1]Quoted in Richard Foster, *Prayer: Finding the Heart's True Home* (San Francisco: HarperSanFrancisco, 1992), p. 255.

[2]This line originally appeared in a cartoon in *Leadership Journal,* October 1, 2001 <www.ctlibrary.com/le/2001/fall/9.53.html>.

[3]Bruce D. Perry and Maia Szalavitz, *The Boy Who Was Raised as a Dog: And Other Stories from a Child Psychologist's Notebook: What Traumatized Children Can Teach Us About Loss, Love and Healing* (Cambridge, Mass.: Basic Books, 2006), pp. 230-32.

[4]Michael Downey, *Altogether Gift: A Trinitarian Spirituality* (Maryknoll, N.Y.: Orbis, 2002), p. 41.

[5]Jean Vanier, *From Brokenness to Community* (Mahway, N.J.: Paulist Press, 1992), p. 23.

[6]Ibid., p. 19.

[7]Quoted in Frances M. Young, *Brokenness and Blessing: Towards a Biblical Spirituality* (Grand Rapids: Baker Academic, 2007), p. 94.

[8]Simone Weil, *Waiting for God* (New York: Perennial Classics, 2001), p. 65.

[9]This is adapted from my book *Holy Fools: Following Jesus with Reckless Abandon* (Carol Stream, Ill.: Tyndale House, SaltRiver Press, 2008), pp. 84-87.

[10]This phrase is from a sermon of John Chrysostom, *Baptismal Instructions* (New York: Newman Press, 1963), p. 115.

Conclusion: Prayer as Praying

[1]Søren Kierkegaard, *Provocations* (Farmington, Penn.: Plough Publishing, 2002), p. 354.

Scripture Index